REVOLT
against
REALITY

Fighting the Foes of Sanity and Truth—

from the Serpent to the State

GARY MICHUTA

Catholic
Answers
Press

Published by Catholic Answers, Inc.
2020 Gillespie Way
El Cajon, California 92020
1-888-291-8000 orders
619-387-0042 fax
catholic.com

Printed in the United States of America
Cover design by Claudine Mansour Design
Cover art, Adam and Eve, by Lucas Cranach the Younger
Interior by Russell Graphic Design

978-1-68357-252-7
978-1-68357-253-4 Kindle
978-1-68357-254-1 ePub

Contents

IV.
EPISTEMOLOGICAL REVOLT

V.
SOCIAL REVOLT

Acknowledgments

There are so many people I'd like to thank for their advice and support for this book. Richard O'Bannon, Michael Aquilina, Dr. Brian Bradford, Steven Weidenkopf, Dr. Douglas Beaumont, Patrick Flynn, John DeRosa, Drew Belsky, and Todd Aglialoro. My special thanks go to my family for their love and support. Finally, to Sir Arnold Lunn, whose writings inspired me to write this book—may God grant him eternal light and peace.

Introduction

One of my earliest memories as a child was jumping off the front porch of my home, waving my arms, and pretending to fly like a bird. Flights of imagination (forgive the pun) were part of being a child. But today, imagination has taken a strange turn. A fully grown adult can call himself something he's not—even an animal, and even a mythical creature!—and it is heralded as bold statement about how things truly are. Imagination has become transformed into insanity.

The situation we find ourselves in today did not spring out of a vacuum. St. Thomas Aquinas once said a small error in the beginning results in a big error in the end. The insanity of our age, although it may seem unique or just uniquely insane, is simply the outworking of centuries of pushing ancient errors to their logical conclusion. Unfortunately, we find ourselves near the end of this process.

As unfortunate as our position may be, it does afford us a vantage point that our forefathers didn't have. We can trace the history of this present darkness and perhaps chart a course back to sanity.

As we will see, the sources of modern insanity weren't merely errors; they were rebellions against creation and its Creator. We find ourselves at the end point of a revolt against reality, spanning from the beginning of time.

The revolt against reality comprises five acts or movements in history. Each will make up one of five sections within this book: Creation and the Incarnation, Christological Revolt, Ecclesiastical Revolt, Epistemological Revolt, and Societal Revolt.

The Incarnation reveals a vision of reality that transforms and raises Western civilization to heights never before seen by igniting several revolutions of thought and practice. Through these revolutions, a realistic view of the world replaces the errors and fantasies of paganism—what could be described as a true age of reason. This campaign toward sanity, however, encounters resistance and counterattacks along the way.

Since it is impossible to chronicle every aspect of this great drama, we are going to focus on seven battlefield areas of human experience. These are God and Creation, Human Integrity and Value, Marriage and Family, the Church, Community, Government, and Human Knowledge.

Since these are the battlefields that lie before us, it's good to know these areas a little better.

GOD AND CREATION The first battlefield concerns the relationship between the Creator and his creation. How did God create? Was it through his wisdom so that all things are intelligible and we can learn something about their Creator? Or is creation nothing more than God's unconstrained, arbitrary will? Or is there no Creator, and everything is the product of random, purposeless chance?

HUMAN INTEGRITY AND VALUE What is the relationship between body and soul? Where do human dignity and value come from? Are some individuals more human than others?

MARRIAGE AND FAMILY What are the relationships among husbands, wives, and children? What is the nature of marriage?

THE CHURCH What is Christ's Church? Is it an invisible collection of likeminded believers, or is it Christ's mystical body?

COMMUNITY What is the nature of individual relationships within society? How do we treat one another, and how ought we to interact?

GOVERNMENT How ought we to be governed? What is government's proper sphere of influence, and what are its limits?

HUMAN KNOWLEDGE What is the relationship connecting our knowledge of ourselves, history, and the things around us?

Even though we will limit ourselves to these areas, this book is fraught with perils and impossible tasks. For example, it is impossible to avoid generalizations and especially what is called the *single cause fallacy*. This fallacy occurs when one cause is singled out among many as if it were the only cause.

Since we are tracing back in history how we got to our current situation, we will follow the historic thread of only one or two causes because of the impact they will have on later generations. The reader, therefore, should not infer from our silence that other causes weren't at work or ultimately contributed to the revolt we find ourselves in today.

As a final note, the reader ought to approach this work not as a comprehensive Church history, but as a speculative outline that attempts to trace the origin of the present and ever-growing insanity pervading the world.

The overall structure of this work chronicles history from creation to modern times.

In chapters 1–3, we begin with God, his creation, and his original design. We will look at the creation narrative (Gen. 1–2) and highlight certain features that humanity will continually distort or ignore. Humanity falls into barbarism, and God prepares for his definitive revelation of himself.

Chapters 4 and 5 cover the most momentous event in human history—the Incarnation—and the intellectual revolutions it initiates that lead to the creation of Western civilization. On the road to the true age of reason are several counterattacks, detailed in chapters 6–9, that attempt to separate what God joined when he assumed our human nature.

Chapters 10–12 cover how the revolt against reason turns into a full-blown revolution, culminating in the Protestant Reformation. Protestantism begins to strip Christianity of its incarnational character, and its inability to maintain unity ignites religious conflicts throughout Europe, resulting in secularism and modernity.

Chapters 13–15 chronicle how the search for peace, unity, and concord apart from Christ and his Church results in bloodier conflicts, deadly ideology, and the reduction of even the Church to a kind of secret, specialized knowledge.

Chapter 16 covers the rebellion that takes place within Catholicism in the 1960s and its effects on Protestant identity. It also covers the rise of radical feminism, militant egalitarianism, legal positivism, and the gender identity movement.

Finally, chapter 17 surveys the landscape for signs of hope as the revolt against reality is reaching its terminal stages.

This book does not propose a solution to the problems we find today, but it does provide a map of where we came from and where we are heading. It is the author's hope that the reader will find in this broad intellectual and theological survey a path back to sanity and the God of reality.

I.

CREATION AND THE INCARNATION

1

In the Beginning Was Sanity

The Lord God formed man of dust from the ground,

and breathed into his nostrils the breath of life;

and man became a living being.

—GENESIS 2:7

The bizarre and incoherent mess we find ourselves in today didn't happen overnight. It is the result of thousands of years of attacks, counterattacks, victories, and defeats. The drama of this campaign has a strange incoherence about it, like a *man bites dog* story. It is a history of creatures attempting to make their Creator into their own image and likeness. But the most the creature can do is turn away from what truly is and live in a world of his own imagination.

If insanity is measured by the degree to which what one believes corresponds to what truly is, the story of mankind's revolt against reality is really the story of mankind's descent into insanity.

In Defense of Sanity

It's important to say a few words in defense of sanity, since today insanity is portrayed as something fun and entertaining.

Let's face it: we love the crazy breakout characters in sitcoms and movies because they spice up an otherwise predictable plot. In real life, however, insanity is not fun at all. In fact, it's not conducive to survival. If you truly believe that a fruit is safe to eat when it is actually poisonous, you'll die. Likewise, if you believe that gravity doesn't apply to you and you jump off a roof, bad things will result. Reality ultimately has the final word.

Sanity produces the opposite. When you see things as they truly are (and live accordingly), good things result. Sanity invariably leads to human flourishing, whereas its opposite alienates us from ourselves and from all that is around us— to regression, human misery, and destruction.

This alone accounts for the strange paradox we are experiencing in Western culture. The people who believe that the 1960s ushered in an era of unprecedented freedom and sexual liberation are among the angriest and the most miserable people you'll meet. As of 2019, suicide was the fourth leading cause of death in the United States for people ages thirty-five to fifty-four and the second cause of death for those between the ages of ten and thirty-four.[1]

How is it that with all the modern age's material wealth, freedom, and liberation, suicide should be so popular? The fact is that we are on the wrong side of the revolt against reality.

GOD AND CREATION

The Word Creates

"In the beginning God created the heavens and the earth" (Gen. 1:1).

The first verse of the Bible stands out. God created the heavens and the earth. Then what?

The early Church Fathers saw Genesis 1:1 as the "first creation." God creates all things instantaneously out of nothing (*ex nihilo*). The rest of the creation narrative (called the *second creation*) speaks of how God gives everything form and structure.[2]

Creation wasn't a random, unintelligible mishmash of stuff thrown together or broken apart, like the Babylonian *Enûma Eliš* myth. God imparts order, structure, and form. The cosmos is reasonable and intelligible because God, who is wisdom itself, created it that way.

There is a deep order to creation. For example, there is a hierarchy of beings: sun, moon, stars; vegetation, sentient animals, and then rational animals (Adam and Eve). Each has its proper place and dominion, with man and woman in the privileged spot.

Within each of these levels, God creates an order within the order. The plants and animals are not made indiscriminately; the text repeats how he made them "according to their kind." Each has a distinctive nature and can do what is proper to that nature. Fruit-bearing plants, for example, can bear the kind of fruit proper to their nature. Although each plant is separate and distinct in its own way, nevertheless, they can be seen collectively "according to their kinds," a phrase that is repeated ten times in only five verses (Gen. 1:21–25).

Adam and Eve are both part of God's creation and yet unique in it. They have dominion over all the creatures of the earth. Unlike the animals below them, they are made in the image and likeness of God. He creates them male and female. Although *male and female* is not exclusive to humanity, there is still something unique with men and women, a special complementarity that exists between them.

HUMAN INTEGRITY AND VALUE
Ensouled Bodies

Genesis also says something about the human person. God took dust from the ground and shaped Adam's body and blew into it the breath of life (Gen. 2:7). Adam comprises two different things: a body and a living soul. The body came from the earth, and God directly created and infused the soul. This means that Adam is not two things (body and spirit) dwelling together like a *ghost in the machine*, but a body-soul composite.[3] His inanimate material body became alive through the "breath of life." The unity of body and soul is such that one affects the other; the soul informs the body, and what we do in the body affects the soul.

Being made in the image and likeness of God—having intellect and will—every human being is priceless, not because of what he does, but because of what he is: a created icon of God.

It Is Not Good for Man to Be Alone

Throughout the creation narrative, the text repeatedly states that "God saw that it was good" (Gen. 1:10, 12, 18, 21, 25), but on the sixth day, "God saw everything that he had made, and behold, it was very good" (v. 31). Then the pattern is broken when God says: "It is not good that the man should be alone; I will make him a helper fit for him" (Gen. 2:18). God puts Adam to sleep and fashions Eve from his side—equal to Adam in dignity, made equally in the image of God, from the beginning.

Adam expresses the built-in complementarity and unity between man and woman like this: "This at last is bone of my bones and flesh of my flesh; she shall be called woman, because she was taken out of man" (Gen. 2:23). Although Adam and Eve are distinct individuals, they are united in a one-flesh bond that no other kind of creature can duplicate.

MARRIAGE AND FAMILY
One-Flesh Union

This one-flesh unity, the narrator of Genesis notes, is the origin of the mysterious union of a man and woman in marriage, "therefore a man leaves his father and his mother and cleaves to his wife, and they become one flesh" (Gen. 2:24). The profound union of matrimony is such that husband and wife no longer remain two distinct people. Rather, they are one flesh, the same substance. Once made, this bond can never be dissolved.

THE CHURCH
Groom and Bride

We also find here, in the garden, the Church in seed form. Adam is the covenant head, who receives God's law (Gen. 2:15–17), and God gives him a duty to instruct his bride in that law.

HUMAN KNOWLEDGE
Knowing God

There is also something important not explicitly mentioned in Genesis 1–2, but it is certainly there. Our first parents had—and we have, too—unbounded desires that can never be truly satisfied with any created thing, even if it were paradise itself, since these are only limited, imperfect reflections of what is found in God.

The source of our first parents' happiness extended far beyond anything found in the garden of paradise. Their ultimate happiness and fulfillment were to be found in the one who made them in his image and likeness.

We all possess an innate desire for perfect truth, love, justice, beauty, and home. Since these desires go beyond anything here on earth, they are called *transcendental desires*. Not only do all humans have them, but we notice the world's inability to fulfill them.

Toddlers, with their incessant "why," are a great example of this awareness. When a parent answers, the child demands a deeper explanation. After several cycles of this, the parent becomes frustrated and answers something like, "Because I say so!" or "Stop pestering me!" As adults, we know that only

God can provide the complete, total answer to any question. The toddler knows it, too, on some level—and he asks his parents on earth, just as we might ask our Father in heaven.

The toddler will eventually learn that his parents don't know everything. Nor will they be able to satisfy his ultimate desire. Only God, who is wisdom itself, can satisfy this desire—not only for perfect truth, but also for perfect love, justice, goodness, beauty, and unity.

Why do we have these desires? St. Augustine most perfectly explains: "You have made us for yourself, O Lord, and our heart is restless until it rests in you."[4] Since God loves us and created us, the fulfillment of all our desires is to be found in him alone.

The Directedness of Creation

Earlier, we saw how God made each thing according to its proper nature or kind. What something is gives it a capacity to act in a certain way. Each nature has the potential to do some things and not others. In other words, a thing's nature is directed toward some goal or range of goals. An apple tree is directed toward producing apples, not gorillas. Philosophers call the study of this kind of directedness *teleology*.

God didn't create everything and then let it spin into chaos. God in his wisdom created all things with proper natures so creation would be directed and orderly.

Since all things have a directedness about them, there are also *secondary causes*. Picture a cue ball being directed toward the four ball on a pool table. What made the four go into the pocket? The cue ball struck it. What caused the cue ball to strike the four? The pool player directed it with the pool cue. God sometimes intervenes directly in creation through miracles (like hitting the cue ball with a pool cue), but he more often uses the directedness he built into nature. By creating animals and plants according to their own nature or kind, he does not have to continually intervene in creation from one generation to another. He can frontload his will into the nature of things so they bring about his desired results through their natural capabilities.[5] All the while, God continuously holds all things in existence, maintains their nature, and supplies the power for this directedness to exist.

The picture Genesis 1–2 gives us is that all of creation is a finite reflection of the wise Creator who created it, especially our first parents. But there was another rational creature in the garden, who will initiate the revolt against reality.

2

The First Revolt

But the serpent said to the woman,

"You will not die."

—GENESIS 3:4

In the third chapter of Genesis, the diabolical serpent disrupts the harmony of God's creation:

> Now the serpent was more subtle than any other wild creature that the Lord God had made. He said to the woman, "Did God say, 'You shall not eat of any tree of the garden'?" And the woman said to the serpent, "We may eat of the fruit of the trees of the garden; but God said, 'You shall not eat of the fruit of the tree which is in the midst of the garden, neither shall you touch it, lest you die.'" But the serpent said to the woman, "You will not die" (vv. 1–4).

What the serpent says doesn't correspond with how things truly are. This is the first recorded act of insanity: the lie.

Mistaken Appearances

The devil's lie implies that creation isn't as it appears: God's law only *appears* to be good, but it really isn't. *God's law is holding you down.* The serpent's sales pitch ends with the false promise that if Eve partakes of the forbidden fruit, "your eyes will be opened, and you will be like God, knowing good and evil" (Gen. 3:5).

In this context, knowing good and evil doesn't mean recognizing things as good and bad. Adam and Eve already can do that. The serpent means that they will "know" good and evil *as God knows* good and evil. How does God *know* good and evil? God knows himself, who is goodness itself. And the good God created all things good. The serpent is essentially telling Eve that if she and Adam eat of the fruit, *they* will be the ones who determine whether something is good or evil.

HUMAN INTEGRITY AND VALUE
Mind and Will Disoriented

Since God constituted human beings as body-soul composites with the capability of knowing and freely willing, the harmony between knowing what truly is and acting in accord with it would continue as long as they remained faithful to the Creator. When Adam and Eve believe the serpent's lie and sin, the integrity of their knowledge and will becomes distorted. Knowing and doing are no longer oriented toward God. The intellect becomes darkened, and the will bends away from God.

Human integrity is shattered in another way. Through the devil's envy, death enters the world. In death, the body and soul are separated, and human bodies—made to be temples of God—are buried and suffer corruption (Wis. 2:23–24).

Unfaithful Bride

Did you ever wonder why the serpent approaches Eve and not Adam? Adam is the real target. If the devil can get Adam to rebel against the Creator, he can corrupt humanity at its root. Instead, he approaches Eve.

The early fathers saw a malevolent logic being played out in the devil's choice of approach.[6] The devil gains a twofold advantage in that he can capitalize on the fact that it is not good for man to be alone. If the devil can get Eve to join his rebellion against God, Adam will have to make a choice: follow his helpmate in rebellion, or be alone once again.

The second advantage is that God gave the command not to eat to Adam before the creation of Eve (Gen. 2:17). It's not written that God ever repeated his command, yet Eve knows it almost word for word. How did she learn it? The Church Father Irenaeus proposes that she learned it from Adam.[7] The serpent's lie strikes at Eve's trust in her spouse, the covenant head. Her sin, therefore, is as much a vote of no confidence in Adam as a rebellion against God.

Secret Knowledge, Divine Deception

As we noted earlier, Adam and Eve also represent the Church in seed form, since Christ's relationship with the Church is that of a bridegroom with his bride. In this the serpent's lie foreshadows later rebellions, such as the introduction of secret knowledge. The lie is a claim to disclose something about God that was not revealed to Adam or taught to Eve.

Satan's lie essentially is a claim that the normal order of things, and even God's law, does not reflect how things truly are. According to the serpent, God's commands are ordered not to our first parents' perfection, but to their repression. The devil proposes that the good God doesn't always act in a good way. In other words, he separates *what God is* (goodness itself) from *what God wills.*

Eve has a choice: trust Adam (and the goodness of God), or place her trust in the serpent's secret knowledge. She unwisely chooses the latter. Believing the lie, she and her husband partake of the fruit and commit to the most insane belief possible: that goodness itself does not always act good.

As with every insane act, our first parents' rebellion has consequences. Adam and Eve lose their original glory. God banishes them from paradise, and they experience death and corruption. They have to labor for whatever fruit they produce, whether it is food from the earth or children from the womb. Humanity falls out of step with reality and suffers because of it.

Where once God walked in their presence, now Adam and Eve, and all their children, wander the earth with the wound of their insane act. Now humanity's intellects are darkened, and their wills are inclined toward evil. They are estranged from each other and estranged from God.

But God has not abandoned them. Instead, he begins the slow process of restoring humanity to its senses.

3

Baby Steps Back to Reality

I will again pour out teaching like prophecy,

and leave it to all future generations.

—SIRACH 24:33

The fall of our first parents is steep, and it dramatically affects their offspring from the start. The first child mentioned in Scripture is Cain. Born in exile from Eden, Cain slays his brother, Abel, and tries to hide his crime. So Adam's first offspring commits fratricide, and things only get worse from there. Mankind spreads and splinters, becoming blood-thirsty and warlike. Despite this, God never abandons us. He begins his work by choosing for himself a group of people who will be separated and distinct from the rest.

Although they too are fallen and sinful, God will teach and train this group, slowly rehabilitating them and rein-troducing sanity, one small step after another, purifying their minds and hearts so they will be ready for his fullest revelation of himself in the Messiah and Son of God, Jesus Christ.

Atheists sometimes argue that if God does exist, he should have bestowed upon the most ancient people the perfect law, taught them about science—basically, given them all the answers in the back of the book—instead of teaching them barbaric things like the *lex talionis* ("an eye for an eye and a tooth for a tooth") and legislating divorce when we learn later that divorce is wrong. For atheists, God seems not to be reintroducing sanity, but rather to be introducing more barbarism.

But had God given his perfect law from the beginning, it would have immediately failed. Humanity had to learn with great difficulty the fundamentals before it could be ready for the perfect law. This is true for all areas of life. A student cannot learn calculus without first learning the basic elements of mathematics. Likewise with theology and morality. God giving the perfect revelation of himself immediately after the fall would be like giving a toddler a calculus textbook. He might use it as a toy, but he won't comprehend it.

Moreover, human beings are not computers. We don't download information like a program and then flawlessly perform its commands. Principles need to be instilled in us and habits formed. Think back to your earlier days in school. It may have taken you a month or two (or even a whole semester) to learn a formula or several key axioms. They require repetition, or they are quickly forgotten. If you don't use it, you lose it.

We also tend to remember truths better when they are discovered rather than learned through instruction. A parent may tell his child dozens of times not to stick his finger in an electrical socket, but it takes only one shock for a child to learn this command and flawlessly obey it for the rest of his life. It is only after certain elemental truths and principles are so engrained that to do otherwise would be unthinkable that it is time to move to tackling more advanced principles.

There is also the matter of virtue. Computers slavishly follow the dictates of their programs, but we can reject what we know to be true. It's easy to dismiss truths as false or doubtful if they are difficult or uncomfortable to live out. Virtue is needed to embrace what is true and reform our lives accordingly. It is only through continuous practice that a virtue becomes a habit. Habits form character, and people of virtuous character transform culture. Once a virtuous culture is formed, it takes on a kind of momentum that promotes further virtuous behavior and habits and people of character.

Fallen human nature cannot skip any of these steps. Training must begin by lifting lighter weights before moving to heavier ones. Therefore, God stoops down to our level, dealing with the most primitive people as they are, so they can understand and grow in virtue. By building, principle upon principle, and virtue upon virtue, he reintroduces sanity into the world. This process is what the Old Testament records.

But, someone may say, how can barbarities be virtuous? Take Leviticus 24:20: "Fracture for fracture, eye for eye, tooth for tooth; as he has disfigured a man, he shall be disfig-ured." What's right about this law is that it introduces the idea of proportionate response. In the ancient world, there was no such universal recognition. Tyrants did whatever they wanted and whatever it took to instill fear in their enemies and their subjects.[8] No limits. If a person injured your eye, you could burn his house down—that is, if you were strong enough to get away with it. Proportionate response teaches that a pun-ishment should be in proportion to the crime. Today, it may seem barbaric, but back when it was introduced, it was quite enlightened. As culture was transformed and elevated, its application became more refined until today, when the literal application of *eye for eye* would be unthinkable.

Some disordered behavior is so deeply rooted in fallen humanity that initial steps had to be taken to limit the evil before it could be banned outright. Take divorce. With-out the prerequisite training in virtue and grace, banning divorce could have resulted in the primitive Israelite men murdering their undesirable wives. Therefore, legislation was made to permit and regulate divorce. Once these regu-lations had become instilled within the culture, the thought of murdering one's spouse became unthinkable, and the road was open for the introduction of the perfect law of lifelong marriage. The same is true for other evils, such as slavery. The evil was regulated and restricted until the stage was set for its abolition.

God's people advance slowly. Many times, they take two steps forward only to take one step back. Although not perfect, they do separate themselves from the nations. They persevere in monotheism, although they do have to return to it regularly after frequent failures.

God Outside Israel

God is also active during this time with those outside Israel. He providentially prepares them, too, for the definitive revelation of himself.[9] Despite the pagan nations' fall into the irrational worship of idols, there remains a worldwide belief, albeit often obscure and combined with errors, in a supreme deity (Rom. 1:20–24). As author Roy Varghese points out:

> While primitive animism and nature deities can be easily explained as attempts to personalize the forces of nature, the same cannot be said of the concept of a Supreme Being. It is entirely abstract, with no physical or imaginative correlate; and yet it came naturally to humans throughout history.[10]

This belief in an immaterial supreme deity isn't the product of imagination, fear, or some physical phenomenon. It comes from another source. Scholars call this intrinsic awareness *the numinous*. It is found everywhere, even among the most secluded primitive cultures who have no contact with the outside world.[11]

During the fourth century B.C., God's Providence works a miracle among the pagans. That miracle will revolutionize

Western thought, complete the preparation for God's definitive revelation to his people, and prepare the way for the explosive growth of Christianity.

The Greek Miracle

The Greek miracle is threefold. Greek philosophy has developed to the point where those among its greats—Plato and Aristotle especially—have succeeded in recognizing the Creator through unaided human reason. This recognition is by no means perfect. Even Aristotle's Prime Mover is faulty in many respects.[12] Nevertheless, Greek philosophers begin to speculate about a Divine Reason or Word (Gk., *Logos*) creating and ordering all things. They notice how immaterial entities like abstractions, universals, numbers, and geometry apply consistently and reliably to the material world. They begin to catalogue plants and animals according to their *genera* or kind (remember Genesis 1?). In other words, Greek philosophy has paved the way to understand, in a profound way, the Creator through the things he has made. These philosophical developments will later provide a bridge that Christian revelation uses to spread the gospel through the Western world.

I don't wish to paint too rosy a picture. Even the best philosophers' understanding of reality was distorted, including such perversions as polytheism, cyclical time, and an eternal cosmos, just to name a few. However, they did come close enough to the mark that some Jewish and early Christian writers accused the Greeks of plagiarizing Moses.

Judaism Encounters the Greeks

Alexander the Great (356–323 B.C.) contributes to the second part of the Greek miracle. He brings about a program of Hellenization to the lands he conquers. This means a common language uniting the ancient Western world. Hellenization also introduces Greek culture, thought, and practices to every corner, including Judaea.

After Alexander's death, the empire is divided into four parts: Macedonia, Ptolemaic Egypt, the Seleucid Empire, and the Kingdom of Pergamon. Judaea falls under the Seleucid Empire.

The Seleucids are initially successful in forcibly Hellenizing Judaea. However, the Jews wage a campaign of armed resistance, led by the Maccabees, between 167 and 160 B.C. It is during this time that we find—for the first time in Jewish history—Jews willing be to martyred rather than transgress the commandment of God (see 2 Macc. 6–7).

Wisdom and Word

It is during this period that one of the most remarkable developments takes place in Jewish thought: a sharpening of the understanding of God's wisdom. God's wisdom is seen as being with God and yet also God himself. It is described as his Word, the creative Word that he spoke in the beginning that brought all things into existence:

I came forth from the mouth of the Most High, and covered the earth like a mist. I dwelt in high places, and my

throne was in a pillar of cloud. Alone I have made the cir-
cuit of the vault of heaven and have walked in the depths
of the abyss. In the waves of the sea, in the whole earth,
and in every people and nation I have gotten a possession
(Sir. 24:3–6).

The biblical books of Proverbs and Sirach retell the story
of creation from Genesis 1, only God's Word is not presented as an impersonal command. Rather, it is personified.
Proverbs 8 speaks of Wisdom as being "beside" God before
creation, like a craftsman. In Sirach, Wisdom is seated on
his throne on a pillar of cloud, the same kind of pillar of
cloud where the Almighty sits (see Exod. 19:9, 33:9–10).[13]
God's Word, like God himself, encompasses heaven and the
deep. The Word also dwells in a special way in a particular
geographic location: Israel.

The book of Wisdom also describes God's Wisdom
(Word) as "unique" or "only-begotten" (Greek, *mongenes*),
which, as we will see in the next chapter, is an important
philosophical term.[14] Wisdom is not only personified in this
book, but also given divine attributes such as being "all-
powerful" and "overseeing all" (7:23).[15]

Another important development is the solution to a
Greek riddle of abstractions: how can our minds see things
that don't exist concretely in the world around us, such as
numbers, geometry, and universals? Plato thought our mind
sees them because our souls remember them from a previous
existence. The book of Wisdom counters that the wise God

arranged and disposed all things to be understood "by measure and number and weight" (Wis. 11:20).

The Greek Septuagint

The final aspect of the Greek miracle is the Septuagint. Around 250 B.C., the Jewish scriptures are translated into Greek. According to the *Letter of Aristeas*, King Ptolemy sends a request to the high priest, Eleazar, that seventy-two scholars of the law translate the Scriptures from Hebrew into Greek. The high priest complies, which eventually results in what we call the Greek *Septuagint* (or seventy, LXX).

The Septuagint marks a dramatic change in salvation history. Up until this time, the Israelites were a people unto themselves. Their identity was to be separate and distinct, and their religious focus was on practicing righteousness. With the Septuagint, the Greek-speaking nations now have access to God's revelation. Since Greek has become the common tongue of the ancient Western world, anyone who is literate can access the Law and the Prophets. It soon becomes a popular translation for the Jews as well, both in Judaea and throughout the diaspora.

All this sets the stage for the great unifying moment in human history: when the Creator enters into creation, the invisible becomes visible, and God assumes human nature and elevates it, bringing together faith and reason, Jew and Greek, indeed all of humanity into one body. The subject of the Greek philosophers' speculation is about to become reality, walking in the streets of Judea.

4

Wisdom Becomes Flesh

But when the time had fully come,

God sent forth his Son, born of a woman.

—GALATIANS 4:4

Shortly before the beginning of the first Christian century, Judaism has reached a new point in its development, which the New Testament calls "when the fullness of time had come" (Gal. 4:4, NRSV:CE). The rise and the fall of Alexander the Great and the subsequent Hellenization of the ancient world is slowly giving way to the Roman Empire with its sophisticated military, legal, and transportation systems. Judaism has also reached a point where Jews are willing to die rather than to violate the Law. Their Scripture has been translated into the *lingua franca* of the nations, and its latter books have moved Jewish revelation to the brink of what will later become a trinitarian understanding of God.

All this lays the groundwork for the most important point in human history: the Incarnation. The Incarnation is when

God's Word takes on our human nature while remaining God.

It's difficult to express the profundity of the Incarnation. When the Word takes on our flesh, heaven and earth are united. The one transcendent God comes near us. The invisible God becomes visible. The things of the earth become instruments of the divine. The goodness of the body is affirmed. Death is defeated. A radically realistic view of time and space is revealed. Matrimony is restored in its purity. And God's people can now enter into a one-flesh union with Christ in a most profound and mysterious way.

GOD AND CREATION
Reunion and Union

It is through the Incarnation that the Creator enters his creation to communicate himself to us in the most real, tangible way possible, as true man, through faith and the sacraments.[16]

This intimate union is foreign to the pagan worldview. The pagans live in an incoherent, dreamlike world marked by superstition and a multitude of gods. These gods are fickle and brutal, rarely caring about human affairs, dwelling apart from humanity.

The greatest and most sophisticated pagan philosophers saw something more. Over and above all these fickle gods was *the One* who maintained the cosmos for all eternity. The One was remote and cold. Unlike the anthropomorphic lower gods—who were worshipped and feared in part because of their unpredictability—the One was most reasonable and most hidden.

The Jewish view of God is similar. Although he loves and is with his people, he nevertheless is above and beyond creation, dwelling in the highest of heavens in unapproachable light, never revealing his form. This is why making images of God is forbidden (Deut. 4:12–20).

The Incarnation radically changes this view. The one transcendent God of Israel takes on flesh, has a name, and walks the earth. As St. John's prologue states:

> In the beginning was the Word, and the Word was with God, and the Word was God. He was in the beginning with God; all things were made through him. . . . And the Word became flesh and dwelt among us, full of grace and truth; we have beheld his glory, glory as of the only Son [Greek, *monogenous*; "only-begotten"] from the Father (John 1:1–5, 14).

To the first-century Jewish reader, John's prologue is shocking because he is saying God's Word—the Wisdom of God, the all-overseeing, all-powerful brightness of eternal light—walks the earth as a man! For the first-century philosophically minded pagan, John's prologue says something just as shocking: the only-begotten of God created the cosmos and is known and knowable.

In ancient Greece the word *monogenes* referred to the eternally emanating cosmos. . . . To Plato, for instance, the *monogenes* was the unknown god, the cosmos itself.

Plotinus, six hundred years after Plato, still referred to the *monogenes* as the unknown god.[17]

It's possible that, for this reason, St. Paul chose to preach about "the God who made the world and everything in it" at the shrine dedicated "to an unknown god" in Athens (Acts 17:23–24).

The Image of the Invisible God

God now relates to humanity in a different way. In times past, God did not show his form, but with the Incarnation, God reveals himself in Christ. Jesus is the *image* (Gk., *eikōn*) of the invisible God (Col. 1:15). He can now be represented through images. Christ's true humanity can be depicted in art, especially through its physiological realism, and Christ's divinity can be written in icons, through which the mind is raised to contemplate the divine person.

Even more important, the Incarnation makes it possible for us to learn directly about God through our senses. The first Christians learn about God by seeing, hearing, and touching Jesus. By assuming human flesh, God reaffirms the goodness of physical creation.

Sacramentality

God unites divinity and humanity, and physical matter becomes a medium through which God acts. Indeed, Christ works miracles through his human body. Audible commands uttered by his vocal cords scatter demons and heal the sick, deaf, and blind. Christ's garment becomes the instrument through which a sick woman is instantaneously healed (Mark 5:31; Luke 8:45). Christ even heals with mud and saliva (John 9:6). He feeds the multitude with a few barley loaves, fish, and prayer (see Matthew 14:19ff; Mark 6:38ff; Luke 9:16ff; John 6:9ff).

Christ also institutes seven specific ways through which supernatural effects are manifested. They use material things such as water and oil and specific actions such as words and the laying on of hands. They are baptism, penance, confirmation, the Eucharist, matrimony, holy orders, and the anointing of the sick. These outward signs that produce invisibly what they signify are called *sacraments*.

HUMAN INTEGRITY AND VALUE
Affirming the Body

Not only is physical matter now capable of being used for divine purposes, but the goodness of the human body is profoundly reaffirmed. For us today, this doesn't seem like a big deal, but for the ancients, it is revolutionary.

Before Christ, it was a person's soul, not the body, that was good. The body was the seat of pain, suffering, and the passions. Some, like Heraclitus, believed that the body was "more worthless than dung."[18] For people like Plato, death was almost to be celebrated since it liberated the soul from the imprisonment of the body.[19] The idea of a bodily resurrection, therefore, seemed ridiculous to pagans. As N.T. Wright points out in his exhaustive work on resurrection:

Christianity was born into a world where its central claim was known to be false. Many believed that the dead were non-existent; outside Judaism, nobody believed in resurrection.[20]

Pagan ideas about the afterlife varied. Some believed in reincarnation, with the cyclical prison it entails; others thought the soul loses its identity or perhaps lives somewhere in a dark, shadowy, and scary realm. None of these views allowed the possibility of the soul *returning into the same body*.

The Incarnation, the Resurrection, and the glorification of Christ's body concretely affirm the goodness of both the body and the soul. This belief has several important implications:

The human body is an essential part of the human person, not a shell to be discarded but a product of God's good creation. In the end, it is the whole human person who receives salvation, not the "spiritual" part only. Christian salvation is not a disembodied cosmic union with the divine that results in the absorption of the individual into God and the individual's loss of self. God cares for the whole person, whom he created in his image, and whom he loves enough to save for an eternal relationship.[21]

The implications of the Incarnation (divinity united to humanity, the invisible becoming visible, material things becoming the instruments used for divine purposes, the goodness of the body and the soul) change the course of human destiny—both for mankind and for every individual.

Death Defeated

Given paganism's low view of the body, it is no surprise that pagans found the bodies of the dead utterly repulsive. The sight of them displeased the gods, and they were disposed of far away from the city centers. Even in Judaism, where proper respect and burial of the dead are highly prized, touching a corpse made a person ritually unclean.

For Christians, the body is seen as a temple of the Holy Spirit. Their bodies as well as their souls are sanctified, empowered by grace, members of Christ, and made for glory in heaven. Death does not separate the Christian from God, nor does it separate him from the community:

> The first visible Christian structures were the catacombs. In the catacombs the Christians buried their dead and celebrated the "birthdays" of the martyrs. They surrounded their loved ones with the most elaborate and costly art they could afford—sometimes mere graffiti, but in some cases, they produced some of the most striking paintings that have survived from ancient times. The more martyrs there were, the more often Christian assembled in the catacombs.[22]

Christians move the cemeteries into their cities and even place the remains of the martyrs near the center of worship, below the Christian altar.

Saints and Relics

Since Christ's Incarnation inaugurates the sacramental principle of God producing spiritual benefits through physical things, the same principle applies to the bodies of the saints. God can produce miracles through holy men and women. Since it's God who produces such things, he can do so whether they are alive on earth or in heaven. It is the Incarnation that brings about the early Christian practice of venerating relics and other such things.

Some may dispute this. "Relics, an early authentic Christian practice! Nonsense. Venerating relics and honoring saints crept into the Church through pagan influence!" However, in *The Cult of the Saints: Its Rise and Function in Latin Christianity*, Peter Brown shows that the situation is quite the opposite. Honoring saints and venerating their relics is a distinctly *Christian* practice. The way Christians embraced death was abhorrent to the pagan worldview. We can tell when a location became Christian precisely when the cemeteries were moved into the cities and there was veneration of the remains of the martyrs.

Just as the Incarnation unites heaven and earth, the bodies of the saints—who are closest to God while here on earth—are still beloved of God in heaven. Therefore, God continues to perform great works through them:

> Wherever their relation with the ecclesiastical hierarchy, the Christian Mediterranean and its extension to the east and northwest came to be dotted with clearly indicated *loci* when heaven and earth met. . . . As Gregory of Nyssa

said, "Those who behold them embrace, as it were, the living body in full flower: they bring eye, mouth, ear, all the senses into play, and then, shedding tears of reverence and passion, they address to the martyr their prayers of intercession as though he were present."[23]

The Incarnation not only profoundly unites us to Christ, but also profoundly unites us to each other. This union is expressed through the veneration of relics and the communion of the saints. As David Anders aptly points out:

[What the] Scripture teaches and the Tradition teaches, is this, that the Church is the mystical body of Jesus and in a real sense when I am touching a Christian, I am touching Christ. And even as the sick would touch the body of Jesus and be healed, when I touch Christ in his members I am coming into contact with Christ.[24]

The resurrection of Christ brings about a new certainty about the bodily resurrection. "For if we have been united with him in a death like his [in baptism], we shall certainly be united with him in a resurrection like his" (Rom. 6:5). It is precisely through this Christian incorporation in Christ—in body and soul—that death loses its sting.

Holy Virginity

The reintegrated view of body and soul produces other fruits as well. Christian service—that is, dedicating ourselves to the Lord—takes form. Since we are united as body-soul composites, the body can be seen as the icon or image of the invisible soul. Being a disciple, therefore, isn't purely a spiritual matter; it is also physical.

A single-minded spiritual dedication to the Lord, therefore, can be reflected in the single-minded dedication of the body. For those who are called to it, it means living a life of celibacy. Consecrated virginity reflects this single-minded total gift of self to God (1 Cor. 7:34). The most perfect example of this total dedication is found in the Blessed Virgin Mary, "whose surpassing in purity made her meet to be the mother of the Lord."[25]

The Incarnation also affirms the goodness of the two states of life: holy matrimony (which is raised to a sacrament) and celibacy. The first is ordered to the generation of children. The second is ordered to union with Christ and the supernatural regeneration of and care for the children of God.

Revolution in Meaning

The Incarnation also ushers in a realistic view of the world. Nearly all ancient cultures viewed time as a circle: it has no beginning or end. It just repeats, over and over, so that what we are doing right now will happen again eons from now. Whatever you, or civilization, accomplish today will be wiped out and repeated for all eternity. Indeed, the things you did today, you already had done over and over through the ages.

Such a view has devastating negative implications. If time is an unending repeating cycle, there can never be true progress, only repetition. This is true not only for humans, but for everything.

> In keeping with the mindset of Babylonian and Egyptian cultures, the Greeks also put a strong emphasis on an eternal, cyclic universe and on the comparison of the cosmos to animals. Even the ones with a belief in a monotheistic deity believed that deity was the universe and that all that existed was a cyclic "cosmic treadmill."[26]

But a cosmic treadmill is not only meaningless, but fatalistic. Free will is merely an illusion, since the iron hand of fate rules everything. One person is fated to be great and powerful. Another is fated to be a slave and powerless. All has been predetermined and will repeat for all eternity. No real progress can be made, and nothing can change your lot in life. Caring for the poor, therefore, is futile and absurd, since it is their fate to be poor. Even beliefs in reincarnation or the transmigration of souls cannot effect a change *in this life*. These only give hope that perhaps things will somehow be different in some future life.

Jews and Christians don't share this fatalism. They believe that real change is possible, free will exists, and all is under God's Providence.[27] The possibility of free will, reward and punishment, means that everyone's life—from the poorest slave to the richest king—is a drama with eternal consequences.

MARRIAGE AND FAMILY

Permanence Re-Asserted

We have already discussed matrimony—how Adam and the Eve had a one-flesh union so intimate that he could say of his bride: "This at last is bone of my bones and flesh of my flesh" (Gen. 2:23). However, after the fall, marriage became distorted. Divorce and polygamy soon followed (Gen. 4:23–24). When the fullness of time has come, Jesus reaffirms marriage as it was in the beginning: an exclusive lifelong bond between a man and a woman, ordered to the propagation of offspring. Referencing the legislation of divorce in the Old Covenant, Jesus says:

> But from the beginning of creation, "God made them male and female." "For this reason a man shall leave his father and mother and be joined to his wife, and the two shall become one." So they are no longer two but one. What therefore God has joined together, let not man put asunder (Mark 10:6–9).

Marriage is restored, and it becomes the blueprint for understanding Christ's one-flesh union with his bride, the Church. Husbands and wives remain distinct individuals, yet they are united as one.

THE CHURCH

One Christ, Head and Body

Of all the revolutions the Incarnation will spawn, the most

influential must be our union with God through Christ. Adam's sin had estranged mankind from God and also from one another. The Incarnation radically reversed this by uniting all to himself in a most intimate way—namely, through a one-flesh union like that of a husband and wife (Matt. 19:5–6; Mark 10:8; 1 Cor. 6:16; Eph. 5:31; cf. Gen. 2:24). As Paul teaches:

> Even so husbands should love their wives as their own bodies. He who loves his wife loves himself. For no man ever hates his own flesh, but nourishes and cherishes it, as Christ does the church, because we are members of his body (Eph. 5:28–30).

Did you catch that? The Church, according to Paul, is Christ's own flesh. This one-flesh union is so profound that Christ identifies himself with us in some striking ways. When Saul of Tarsus travels to Damascus to persecute Christians, Christ appears to him, saying, "Saul, Saul, why do you persecute me?" (Acts 9:4).

Christ did not ask Saul, "Why are you persecuting my Church?" or "Why are you persecuting my followers?" or even "Why are you persecuting those who have a personal relationship with me?" He asked, "Why are you persecuting *me*? . . . I am Jesus, *whom you are persecuting*" (Acts 9:4–5, NAB, emphasis mine). We are so intimately united to Christ that when we are persecuted, Christ himself is persecuted.[28]

This union is even exhibited in prophecy. In Galatians 3:16, Paul teaches that *Abraham's seed* can refer to only a single individual, Christ. A few verses later, however, he says all Christians are that same individual seed (Gal. 3:27–29)![29] As Augustine explains:

And for that we too belong to that which is Christ, by our incorporation together, and coherence to that head, it is one Christ. . . . For if the seed of Abraham be one, and that one seed of Abraham can only be understood of Christ; but this seed of Abraham we also are; therefore this whole, that is, the head and the body, is one Christ.[30]

Since there is one Christ—head and body—Abraham's seed refers to Christ alone as head and also to Christ alone as body. Paul likewise teaches elsewhere that Christ crushes the serpent's head, yet all Christians crush him under their feet as well.[31]

Christ's body, the Church, comprises individuals just as a body comprises individual members. Although separate and distinct, they are all united, sharing the same suffering and joy:

For just as the body is one and has many members, and all the members of the body, though many, are one body, so it is with Christ. . . . If one member suffers, all suffer together; if one member is honored, all rejoice together (1 Cor. 12:12, 26).

The analogy of the body also has important implications on the constitution of the Church.

The Incarnation and the Visible Church

The Church is Christ's *body*. A body is a real, physical, tangible, and identifiable thing. It's not invisible, immaterial, or intangible like a soul or a spirit, as Christ himself notes:

> *See my hands and my feet,* that it is I myself; *handle me, and see*; for a spirit has not flesh and bones *as you see that I have* (Luke 24:39, emphasis mine).

If Christ's body is palpable, tangible, identifiable, and structured, so must be his Church. It is a visible, identifiable, ordered society and communion.

The invisible God becomes man so that through his humanity, we will come into fellowship with God. The Church, being Christ's body, extends the Incarnation in time and space. It is by coming into communion with the visible Church—who sees, hears, touches, and believes (see 1 John 1:1–3)—that we come into communion with Christ.

Therefore, it is by having fellowship with *this* community—the body of Christ founded upon the apostles, who heard, saw, and touched him—that one comes into fellowship with the Father and with his Son.

He Who Hears You Hears Me

This fullness of communion with Christ cannot be reduced to writing—even inspired writing—because writings require interpretation. Before the time of Christ, Judaism was divided into various groups, sects, and schools. Each claimed to be the true expression of Judaism, and each had its own distinct opinions and interpretation. When the wisdom of God became flesh, all this was changed:

> [The people] were astonished at his teaching, for he taught them as one who had authority, and not as their scribes (Matt. 7:28–29; see also Mark 1:22; Luke 4:31–32).

It is through the apostolic witness that we come to know Christ and correctly understand the meaning of the inspired Scripture that has come down to us. This can be seen in the pages of the New Testament.

It seems there are some in the early Church who interpret Christ's transfiguration as symbolic or perhaps even a myth. St. Peter's response is telling:

> We did not follow cleverly devised myths when we made known to you the power and coming of our Lord Jesus Christ, *but we were eyewitnesses of his majesty. . . . we heard [God's] voice borne from heaven, for we were with him on the holy mountain.* And we have the prophetic word made more sure. You will do well to pay attention to this as to a lamp shining in a dark place, until the day dawns and the morning star rises in your hearts. First of all you must understand this, that *no prophecy of Scripture is a matter of one's own interpretation*, because no prophecy ever came by the impulse of man, but men moved by the Holy Spirit spoke from God (2 Pet. 1:16, 18–21).

The true interpretation of the Transfiguration is wholly dependent upon apostolic witness. The apostles are eyewitnesses who saw and heard exactly what transpired on Mt. Tabor. Moreover, it is they who possess the prophetic gift of the Holy Spirit, making their testimony normative for Christian belief.

Those who are not disciples of the apostles and do not remain in their teachings are those who twist Scripture to their own destruction (2 Pet. 3:16). As the apostle John wrote:

> We are of God. Whoever knows God listens to us, and he who is not of God does not listen to us. By this we know the spirit of truth and the spirit of error (1 John 4:6).

Conversely, if one does not remain in this community and its teachings, he is a false teacher and out of communion with Christ.

> They went out from us, but they were not of us; for if they had been of us, they would have continued with us (1 John 2:19).

Likewise:

> Any one who goes ahead and does not abide in the doctrine of Christ does not have God; he who abides in the doctrine has both the Father and the Son (2 John 9).

Therefore, the visible apostolic community of the Church is *the* norm for orthodoxy. Those who refuse to remain in the community and its teachings are heterodox or false teachers.

COMMUNITY
"You Did It to Me"

Christ's real identification and union with his body also radically change our relationship with one another. Christ says that at the Final Judgment:

> The King will say to those at his right hand, "Come, O blessed of my Father, inherit the kingdom prepared for you from the foundation of the world; for I was hungry and you gave me food, I was thirsty and you gave me drink, I was a stranger and you welcomed me, I was naked and you clothed me, I was sick and you visited me, I was in prison and you came to me." Then the righteous will answer him, "Lord, when did we see thee hungry and feed thee, or thirsty and give thee drink? And when did we see thee a stranger and welcome thee, or naked and clothe thee? And when did we see thee sick or in prison and visit thee?" And the King will answer them, "Truly, I say to you, as you did it to one of the least of these my brethren, you did it to me" (Matt. 25:34–40).

As Augustine notes:

> But he [Christ] is wont to assume the person of His

members, and to ascribe to himself what should be said of them, because the head and the body is one Christ; whence that saying in the Gospel, "I was hungry, and ye gave me to eat." Expounding which, he says, "Since ye did it to one of the least of mine, ye did it to me."[32]

Christ as head and body brings about a revolution of supernatural charity. The love among the members of his body becomes an extension of our love for the invisible God. 1 John 4:20 reads:

If any one says, "I love God," and hates his brother, he is a liar; for he who does not love his brother whom he has seen, cannot love God whom he has not seen.

"The unseen God is so manifested through Christ's body that to hate a brother in Christ is essentially to hate God. Loving your neighbor becomes not only a salvation issue, but a form of worship and devotion to God."[33] Unlike the Golden Rule that encourages us to treat others as we would like to be treated, Christ instructs us to treat others—especially the poor and needy—as if they were Christ himself.

Supernatural charity also takes on a Christological change with regard to those outside the Christian community and even those who persecute it. We are reminded that Christ died for us even though we are still rebellious sinners (Rom. 5:8). And Christ himself teaches:

You have heard that it was said, "You shall love your neighbor and hate your enemy." But I say to you, Love your enemies and pray for those who persecute you, so that you may be sons of your Father who is in heaven; for he makes his sun rise on the evil and on the good, and sends rain on the just and on the unjust. For if you love those who love you, what reward have you? Do not even the tax collectors do the same? And if you salute only your brethren, what more are you doing than others? Do not even the Gentiles do the same? You, therefore, must be perfect, as your heavenly Father is perfect (Matt. 5:43–48).

The law of Christ introduces something new into the world: the recognition of our common humanity and the necessity to love our enemies (as well as our friends).

Redemptive Suffering

Christians, being united to Christ, live out Christ's life and death in a mysterious way, so that "we suffer with him in order that we may also be glorified with him" (Rom. 8:17).

If one member suffers, all suffer together; if one member is honored, all rejoice together (1 Cor. 12:26).

The suffering of one member of the body can, in virtue of his union with Christ, benefit the whole. As Paul writes:

> Now I rejoice in my sufferings for your sake, and in my flesh I complete what is lacking in Christ's afflictions for the sake of his body, that is, the church (Col. 1:24).

In a mysterious way, Christ's suffering is being lived out in his body so the suffering of one member, Paul, can fill up what is lacking in other members. We see here the groundwork for the idea of indulgences.

HUMAN KNOWLEDGE

Realism Returns

When the Incarnation flattens time, it also opens the door to true scientific progress and eventually modern science as a self-sustaining enterprise.

The Incarnation brings a new realism to history. The Hebrew scriptures recorded history in a sober way, both the good and the bad, chronicling God's providential care for Israel. The New Testament adopts this soberness, but because of the Incarnation, it is focused what those around Jesus see, hear, and say. The Gospels follow the form of an ancient biography, yet they go beyond that. Matthew, for example, focuses on establishing Christ's words and deeds as the fulfillment of Old Covenant prophecy. Like the Hebrew scriptures, the evangelists didn't shy away from telling the truth, even to the point of embarrassment. Miracles are recorded in a factual manner, not to astonish or entertain, like in extra-biblical sources, such as the "miracle accounts" found in the apocryphal *Gospel of Thomas*.

The Genius Of Christianity

Through the Incarnation, the depth, height, and breadth of reality come together and are united. Even extremes and contraries can be seen as one. The highest takes the lowest place. The infinite takes on the finite. He who dwells in unapproachable light, never experiencing suffering and death, suffers and dies. The eternal dwells in time. The Almighty empties himself and makes himself the servant of inferiors.

By uniting humanity to himself, many individuals became one in Christ; each retaining his own individuality and uniqueness, yet all radically one. Each has his own place and function within the body, and like a society, the body has its own internal order and governance, all placed under Christ, the head.

The Incarnation of the Word establishes a beachhead of sanity. From this beachhead, a campaign extends through time and space to re-orientate fallen humanity back to God. This campaign will transform the world.

5

The Incarnation Transforms the Ancient World

As you did it to one of the least of these

my brethren, you did it to me.

—MATTHEW 25:40

The Incarnation is the epicenter of a transformative explosion that sweeps through the cold and barbaric ancient world, spawning new revolutions of thought and practice that lift humanity to new heights. These revolutions are met with resistance from those outside the Church—and, sadly, even from some of those within. The ancient world, nevertheless, is transformed.

GOD AND CREATION
Myths Dispelled

The revelation of Christ shatters pagan misconceptions about the divine. Christ's arrival in history displaces the myth and folklore of pagan mythology and supplies the missing answers raised by the god of the philosophers. It affirms the transcendent God, who is beyond and above all things, while affirming the Creator's intimate connection with creation. These points overtake the errors of animism, which identified God with the world or cosmos, ever changing and repeating, and the cold transcendent One who is unknown and unknowable.

Not Slave, but Brother

As we saw in the last chapter, our radical union with Christ in one body manifests the inherent dignity and value of each person. Applying this *one body in Christ* idea to concrete circumstances revolutionizes how people see one another. You encounter situations where a master and his slave both become Christian. How is the master to relate to his slave? Is he not supposed to treat him as he would Christ? Suddenly, the slave is looked upon no longer as a thing to be used by the master, but as a brother in Christ.

Things become even more odd when one considers that those who are baptized have the right to receive the sacraments, including holy orders. If a slave becomes a priest (usually with the master's permission), the master must now go to his slave to have his children baptized, or to receive the Eucharist, or have his sins forgiven. In fact, two popes, Pius I (d. c. A.D. 155) and Callixtus I (d. 222), will be former slaves. Christianity doesn't abolish slavery as much as it upends it. The process is long and imperfect, but ultimately, unjust title servitude becomes abhorrent and is abandoned, at least for a time.

MARRIAGE AND FAMILY
Property Becomes Persons

Marriage and family also undergo a transformative revolution through the spread of Christianity. This revolution of thought can be appreciated only by understanding how the ancient non-Christian world understood it. We have become so familiar with Christian marriage and family that we suppose that all people everywhere experienced the same thing. Nothing could be farther from the truth. For example, Roman marriage and family life were bereft of love.

> To a Roman man, a wife was property, just as children were property. . . . If no man owned her, she was nobody at all. Children were no better off. Traditionally, a Roman father retained the legal right to execute his children if he judged them guilty of a crime, even into adulthood. They were his children; they belonged to him. . . . From the point of view of Roman tradition, the single most revolutionary thing in Christianity was Paul's startling instruction "Husbands love your wives." . . . After centuries of Christianity we find it hard to imagine that there was a time when husbands weren't supposed to love their wives. Yet, in ancient Rome, a gentleman who obviously loved his wife was sneered at. His wife was his property, not his equal.[34]

The love expressed in Christian marriage transforms the status of women and children by recognizing them as persons, not property.[35] But this is only one aspect of the genius of the Christian revolution.

One for All

The picture of the Church coming out of the first century is a visible identifiable society of disciples, united together as a single body. The unity of this body is such that to be in communion with its members in one location is to be in communion with Christianity as a whole. One early name given to this community is a Greek word *kataholos*, which means "according to the whole" or "universal." That word is still used today—*Catholic*. The historic visible Church will be the touchstone of sanity and a unifying force for every tribe and nation, tongue and sex.

Alms for God

The unity of Christ, head and body, revolutionizes how we look at each other. The love within the Church overflows to all the needy, the downtrodden, the marginalized, even the enemies of the Faith.

Giving to the poor is not unique to Christianity. The Old Testament is replete with commands and encouragements to give alms to the poor (Tob. 4:7–11; 12:8–9; 14:9; Ps. 112:9–10; Prov. 22:9; 28:27; Sir. 3:29; 29:8; 35:2–3; Dan.

4:27). Our Lord echoes this call in several places (Matt. 6:2–3; 19:21; Mark 10:21; Luke 11:41; 12:33; 19:8–9; Acts 10:2). For the Christian, however, giving to the poor and caring for others are ways to love and serve God, since whenever we feed the hungry, clothe the naked, or visit the imprisoned, we do it to Christ. This outflow of love adopts and revolutionizes the Jewish understanding of merit or reward.

Christians and Jews both believe in merit and even a treasury of merit. But why is giving to the poor meritorious before God and beneficial for salvation?

Christian revelation—indeed, the Incarnation—provides the answer. The one Christ is both head and body so that "as you did it to one of the least of these my brethren, you did it to me" (Matt. 25:40; see also 10:40, 42). When we give to the needy, we do it on God's behalf. As Augustine noted, there is a kind of economy of love:

> Study the money-lender's methods. He wants to give modestly and get back with profit; you do the same. Give a little and receive on a grand scale. Look how your interest is mounting up! Give temporal wealth and claim eternal interest, give the earth and gain heaven. "Whom shall I give it to?" did you ask? The Lord himself comes forward to ask you for a loan, he who forbade you to be a usurer (see Matt. 25:34–36). Listen to the Scripture telling you how to make the Lord your debtor, "Anyone who gives alms to the poor is lending to the Lord."[36]

This is a partial quote of Proverbs 19:17, which reads: "He who is kind to the poor lends to the Lord, and he will repay him for his deed."

The unity of Christ's body also transforms this old view of individual merit to a network of love. Since we are all united to Christ, it is no longer we who do these things, but Christ who lives in us (Gal. 2:20). Therefore, when God crowns our merits, he is crowning his own gifts (*Catechism of the Catholic Church*, 2006).

The *treasury of merit* is a component of the idea of indulgences. An *indulgence* is essentially the application of the reward for a good work to benefit a member of the body of Christ, whether for the benefit of the doer or for someone else. The Incarnation and Christ's radical union with his members make this possible.

Philanthrophy Becomes Charity

Christian charity is utterly foreign to the worldview of the ancient Romans and Greeks. Although ancient people placed hospitality at a premium, giving to the poor and helpless was seen as idiocy, unless there was something in it for the donor. Why feed those who are fated to be poor? Christian charity is quite different—done out of love for God and best done in secret (see Matt. 6:2–4).

The Church, being a visible, structured society, can coordinate its charitable efforts, especially to alleviate suffering after a natural disaster.

King Becomes Servant

Another revolution happens in the realm of government. The pagan Roman Empire has been kept together by its superior strength and its cultic unity. In the ancient world, every city had its own protector god or gods. Honoring these gods ordered not only public celebrations, but also the city government.

When the Roman empire took over a city, the Romans didn't suppress its cults or destroy its temples. Instead, the city gods were incorporated into the Roman panoply. The Roman emperor, too, was counted among the deities and given a divine title:

> Julius Caesar claimed to be descended from the gods, and when he died, the Roman Senate proclaimed him divine. Once he was declared to be a god, his nephew and heir, Augustus, claimed to be the son of god. This trend continued until it came to a high point at the end of the first century with the emperor Domitian, who demanded to be called "lord and god."[37]

At first glance, the claim to be a god and demand worship is the twisted byproduct of an overactive ego, but it reveals something else about the emperor. In paganism, the gods did whatever they liked. They were amoral, bloodthirsty, fickle, and imperious. There was no higher law for the gods to obey. Their will was their law. So too with the governments of the ancient world. Outside certain conventions or traditions, there were no demands on how a ruler should rule.

Christians cannot offer sacrifice to Caesar or give him the title of *lord and god* because he isn't the one true God, the Creator of all, whose laws reflect reality. This means that neither the State nor its sovereign is the highest law of the land. Unjust actions of the State are not made just simply because the State says so.[38] There is a higher immutable law that everyone, including the State, ought to follow because it is embedded in the fabric of reality by the one just God.

Christians pray for the emperors (even those who persecute them), and they obey the laws of the land so far as conscience allows. But they insist that all people, including the emperor, have a higher law that must be obeyed.

The Servant King

God, the legislator and Creator of all, humbles himself and becomes man to serve, rather than to be served. The pagan State exists for the preservation of the country and its power, not to serve its citizens. Leadership falls to the victorious. In this era, cutthroat politics and backstabbing are literally that: cutting throats and stabbing backs, although poison seems to be the preferred method. Government is a power grab.

The Incarnation inverts man's expectations. The ruler is to be the servant, and the strong are to be the caretakers of the weak.

Bringing Clarity

The Incarnation introduces a highly realistic view of the world as well as nature's goodness and intelligibility. Christians slowly begin to work in the field of education. They marginalize the superstitious and pernicious elements of the classical works of pagan education while retaining whatever is good or praiseworthy. These Christian educators purify education and the way society views the world.

II.

CHRISTOLOGICAL HERESIES AND THEIR CONSEQUENCES

6

Denial of Christ's True Humanity

We are in a position to reckon up those who were
by the apostles instituted bishops in the churches . . .
who neither taught nor knew of anything like
what these [heretics] rave about.

—ST. IRENAEUS

The sheer brilliance of the Incarnation and its implications
are too much for some to grasp, even within the Church. To
make the Incarnation more palatable, heretics seek to down-
grade either Christ's true humanity or his true divinity.

A modern myth is that the dispute regarding Christ
centered on his divine nature—namely, that Jesus was an
ordinary Jewish teacher and that his followers eventually
elevated him to the status of a god, just as the Roman pagans
elevated their heroes. This promotion to divinity supposedly took place in the fourth century, when the bishops

at the Council of Nicaea made it a dogma. The evidence points in the opposite direction.

At the beginning of the second Christian century, around A.D. 112, the Roman governor Pliny the Younger reports to the Emperor Trajan that Christians "had been in the habit of meeting together on a stated day, before sunrise, and of offering in turns a form of invocation to Christ, as to a god."[39] These invocations are nothing new. The earliest portions of the New Testament contain Christian hymns to Christ that speak about his divinity—for example, Philippians 2:6–11.

It wasn't Christ's divine nature that bothered the pagans. They had all sorts of anthropomorphic gods, and one more didn't matter. The real difficulty was Christ's humanity. Why would the one almighty God—who is incapable of feeling pain, weakness, death—take to himself our human nature, with all these imperfections? God as a philosophical notion is easy to accept. He's distant and abstract. But God made flesh is too real and too realistic. It's a scandal that God would empty himself and take on flesh, suffer, and die. It was not Christ's divinity, but his humanity that provoked the first counterattacks against the Incarnation.

Gnosticism

The apostolic witness of the Church is anchored in Christ's humanity, since it was through the apostles' senses that they learned of Christ's divinity (1 John 1:1). If Christ's humanity is denied, the foundation of Christianity is undermined, and the Faith is transformed into an illusion.

It's impossible to tell when the first denial of Christ's humanity occurred. Some of the later writings of the New Testament appear to confront such denials (1 John 4:2; also 1 Pet. 3:21; 2 John 7). We later hear of the *Docetists*, who claim that Christ only *appeared* to be human, a mere illusion. This implies—like the serpent's lie in the beginning—that we are the victims of divine deception.

Docetism opens the door for an even deadlier heresy that also denies Christ's true humanity, named *Gnosticism*. *Gnostic* comes from the Greek word for "knowledge." The Gnostics, therefore, were the self-proclaimed *knowing ones*.

GOD AND CREATION
Creation Split in Two

The Gnostics, like the pagans, recoil at the thought of God assuming human nature and the bodily resurrection. Gnosticism teaches that the flesh is evil. Material things are to be avoided or rejected, and only immaterial things are good.

Unlike Christianity, Gnosticism is not anchored in reality. It is more of a philosophy or an idea. And since people can come up with new ideas and philosophies, there are many different versions of Gnosticism, all of them too complex to describe here in detail. Most of them use Christian terms like *Christ*, *Logos*, and *Holy Spirit*, but their meanings are radically different.

They generally believe that the material cosmos was produced by an evil god, or *demiurge*, who is opposed by the good god, who created everything spiritual. Obviously, the immaterial good god would never take on the materiality of human nature. Therefore, Christ's humanity must be immaterial or a quasi-material phantom.

Imprisoned Souls

The Gnostics also think, like the pagans, that the good immaterial soul is somehow trapped or imprisoned in a material body. Life's goal, therefore, is to reject the body and material things as much as possible and to adhere to only spiritual things—acquiring secret esoteric knowledge, following special diets, etc.

The Gnostics also hold women in low esteem, unlike Christianity, which exalts the Blessed Virgin Mary as the holiest and most highly venerated human aside from Christ. The Gnostics see males as superior to females, perhaps because women are more biologically (materially) bound to their off-spring. Biology is part of the material world and therefore evil. The redemption for women, therefore, comes by liberating them from the materiality of their sex. As the last line of a Gnostic work called *The Gospel According to Thomas* reads:

> Simon Peter said to them, "Make Mary [probably Magdalene] leave us, for females don't deserve life." Jesus said, "Look, I will guide her to make her male, so that she too may become a living spirit resembling you males. For every female who makes herself male will enter the kingdom of heaven."[40]

Males have to overcome their material bodies. Apparently, females have an extra step. They have to overcome their sex and become male, so they can then overcome the materiality of maleness and enter the kingdom of heaven.

MARRIAGE AND FAMILY
Offspring Avoided

It is not surprising to learn that Gnosticism is inherently anti-procreative. After all, conceiving children only produces more souls trapped in material bodies. Therefore, marriage is frowned upon, since it is ordered to the procreation of children. The idea is to escape the material world, not propagate it.

THE CHURCH
Secret Society

Since the Gnostics reject Christ's real fleshly body, they likewise have difficulty with his body as the visible, identifiable Church. Since they cannot deny the elephant in the room, they do the next best thing by proposing that the Church doesn't fully grasp Christ's teachings. Living up to their name—the *knowing ones*—they claim that Christ and his apostles gave some teachings for the rank-and-file Christians but gave special secret knowledge to the more advanced, which they claim to possess exclusively. Like the serpent's lie, Gnosticism claims a kind of divine deception wrapped up in a conspiracy theory.

It will be Christianity's first theologian, Irenaeus of Lyons, who smashes Gnosticism upon the rocks of reality in the late second century. If there were a real body of secret knowledge, Irenaeus argues, all the Gnostics would believe the same thing, since it all comes from a common source. However, Gnosticism is splintered into many different groups, all teaching bizarre and contradictory things. Such is not the case with the Christian Church:

> It is within the power of all, therefore, in every church, who may wish to see the truth, to contemplate clearly the Tradition of the apostles manifested throughout the whole world; and we are in a position to reckon up those who were by the apostles instituted bishops in the churches, and [to demonstrate] the succession of these men to our own times; those who neither taught nor knew of anything like what these [heretics] rave about. For if the apostles had known hidden mysteries, which they were in the habit of imparting to "the perfect" apart and privily from the rest, they would have delivered them especially to those to whom they were also committing the churches themselves.[41]

If Christianity were a mere belief system, not anchored in a real, visible, physical, identifiable community existing and extending through history, Gnosticism could not be refuted. It would simply be just another belief system, another version of Christianity.

Loss of Unity

Unlike the Gnostics, Irenaeus can demonstrate that the Faith is present throughout the world and can be traced back historically to the apostles. The Gnostics cannot claim such unity and coherence. Earlier, we mentioned that *catholic* means "according to the whole." Gnosticism fails because it isn't catholic in any sense. By denying Christ's humanity, the Gnostics deny that the body of Christ is truly a visible society and insist that it is only a spiritual collection of *knowing ones*. As such, it is little more than an idea, and people can always come up with new ideas.

COMMUNITY
Escaping the Material

Whereas the Incarnation leads Christians to embrace the material world through the sacraments and a sacramental worldview, Gnosticism does the opposite. It reduces salvation to the immaterial acquisition of secret knowledge. Salvation is achieved not by uniting oneself to Christ's body through faith and the sacraments; rather, it is purely an intellectual exercise. The soul is saved, Gnosticism claims, and the body left for dead.

GOVERNMENT
Rulers of the Material Realm

It's not clear how Gnosticism viewed proper government. If later versions of Gnosticism give us a hint, the Gnostics might reject all governmental authority, since it deals with regulating the material world, and the material world is evil. However, Gnostic sects rarely survive long enough to make much of an impact on this issue, since they are sterile: no children, no future.

A Fantasy Replacement

Given that the secret knowledge Gnostics claim to possess is basically a fantasy, the writings they leave behind amount to esoteric and confusing philosophical treatises.

Their anti-material view disinclines them to study nature and scientific thought. Why try to understand the world around us if it was created by an evil god? This is a stark contrast to Christianity, which, because of the Incarnation, has a strong motive to study and contemplate nature and revealed and philosophical knowledge—both of which lead, in their own ways, to the one true God.

Monothelitism

Not everyone denies Christ's true humanity wholesale. Some prefer to deny only aspects of it. These counterattacks against the Incarnation can be more deadly because they are more subtle. For our purposes, we will look at only one such heresy, called *Monothelitism*.

Monothelite means "one will." In the Incarnation, the Second Person of the Trinity, possessing the totality of the one undivided divine substance, assumed our human nature. He is consubstantial with God in terms of his divinity and consubstantial with us in terms of his assumed humanity. That is to say: Christ is like us in all things but sin (Heb. 4:15).

Natures have wills. Therefore, contrary to what the Monothelites claim, Christ has two wills (divine and human) that never contradict each other.

GOD AND CREATION
Did Christ Truly Obey?

The Monothelites never explicitly deny Christ's true human nature, but their insistence that he has only one will opens the door to a demotion of his full humanity to little more than an inanimate instrument of the divine, as some of the more extreme proponents of Monothelitism seem to have held. Christ's humanity, under this view, is little more than a hand puppet of the divine will.

HUMAN INTEGRITY AND VALUE
Did Christ Merit?

Christ's death on the cross is an infinite sacrifice that he offers on our behalf. It's infinite because of his divinity. It's offered on our behalf because of his humanity, as one of us and for all of us. If Christ didn't have a true human will, the second half of this equation would fall apart: Christ wouldn't offer himself as one of us on our behalf, but God would offer an infinite sacrifice to himself as himself. Christ's humanity is reduced to a material thing God used.

Even worse, if Christ didn't have a human will, he couldn't have merited our salvation. In order to merit, to obtain something, one must be able to grow. Christ's divine will cannot merit because it is perfect and thus cannot grow. However, a free human will can. Therefore, Christ's human will enables him to obtain our salvation by merit. For this and other reasons, the Church condemns Monothelitism.

7

Denial of Christ's True Divinity

Owing to the depth of Holy Scripture, all do not accept it in one and the same sense, but one understands its words in one way, another in another; so that it seems to be capable of as many interpretations as there are interpreters.

—ST. VINCENT OF LÉRINS

Gnosticism also opens the door for speculation about Christ's divinity.[42] The heresy of Arianism takes the opportunity to redefine Christ's divinity in a way more acceptable to pagan ears.

Arianism

Arianism is named after the Alexandrian priest Arius (256–336), who wished to emphasize the uniqueness of God the Father by reducing the Son to a demigod.

GOD AND CREATION
The Created Word

The Son, according to the Arians, is not consubstantial and co-eternal with the Father, but created by the Father—so his nature is only *like* the Father's. Arius's formulation is easier to grasp than the true understanding because it is easier to imagine. As Hilaire Belloc notes, "it [Arianism] sprang from the desire to visualize clearly and simply something which is beyond the grasp of human vision and comprehension."[43]

However, imaginings are not the same as reality. Immaterial things cannot be imagined, since our imagination works with only sensible (i.e., material) things.

According to the Arian view, the one true God, the Father, who is uncreated, stands apart from his creation. The Son, who is like the Father, is identified with creation in that he was the first thing created. The Father remains unknowable.

THE CHURCH
Innovations Splinter

Arianism, like all the other counterattacks to the Incarnation, cannot retain unity. The Arians splinter into warring sects like the Gnostics and the other heretics before them. The fifth-century author St. Vincent of Lérins (d. 450), like Irenaeus of Lyons before him, contrasts the splintered heretical sects to the catholicity of the Church of Christ:

Owing to the depth of Holy Scripture, all do not accept it in one and the same sense, but one understands its words in one way, another in another; so that it seems to be capable of as many interpretations as there are interpreters. For Novatian expounds it one way, Sabellius another, Donatus another, Arius, Eunomius, Macedonius, another, Photinus, Apollinaris, Priscillian, another, Iovinian, Pelagius, Celestius, another, lastly, Nestorius another.

Therefore, it is very necessary, on account of so great intricacies of such various error, that the rule for the right understanding of the prophets and apostles should be framed in accordance with the standard of ecclesiastical and Catholic interpretation. Moreover, in the Catholic Church itself, all possible care must be taken, that we hold that faith which has been believed everywhere, always, by all. For that is truly and in the strictest sense Catholic, which, as the name itself and the reason of the thing declare, comprehends all universally.[44]

Just as first-century Judaism comprises competing sects and schools, each claiming to be the true expression of Judaism, those who break from the communion of the apostolic Church splinter into competing factions.

GOVERNMENT
Pontifex Maximus

It is commonly said that once Christianity was legalized in the Roman empire, an influx of pagan converts corrupted the pure Christian Church with their pagan teachings and practices. The fact is that if you compare the writings of

Christians before and after Constantine, you'll find that there wasn't a great apostasy from the true Faith, but rather continuity. If a great apostasy did occur, its name was Arianism, a heresy that Catholics fought vigorously.[45]

As mentioned above, the idea that the Son was a God-like creation is far more palatable to pagan sensibilities than the orthodox view of the Trinity. Christian emperors see this as an advantage and tend to favor Arianism; it appears to soften pagan opposition to Christianity.[46] With the support of a string of emperors, Arianism spreads like a plague throughout the Church until, as St. Jerome (342–420) put it, "the whole world groaned, and was astonished to find itself Arian."[47]

It is only through the determined efforts of saints, like Athanasius (d. 373) and Hilary of Poitiers (310–367), and Church councils like the Council of Nicaea (325), that Arianism is eventually vanquished.

HUMAN KNOWLEDGE
Battling Myths

Despite the influx of Arianism, Christian realism continues to erode and replace the unrealistic worldview of paganism. However, paganism does not go away without a fight. Its last hope for survival comes later, with an emperor known as Julian the Apostate (331–363) and a pagan neo-platonic philosopher named Porphyry (233–305).

8

Paganism Adapts
and Dies

It is disgraceful when no Jew is a beggar

and the impious Galileans support our poor

in addition to their own.

—JULIAN THE APOSTATE

Another counterattack during the long campaign toward a true age of reason comes from the emperor Julian the Apostate (330–363). Julian was born into a Christian family, but he turned against the Faith in a serious way after his family was slaughtered by other family members in a political power play. He was raised by two secret pagans who won him over to the old pagan faith. At the death of Constantius II (317–361), Julian becomes emperor and begins his campaign against Christianity in the hope of restoring paganism to its former glory. By the time Julian becomes emperor, paganism is already on life support. It has lost its supporters to Christianity, and its feasts and celebrations have been largely abandoned.

89

Julian the Apostate

Julian's counterattack is worth considering since aspects of it will resurface in different ways.

There are three components to Julian's anti-Christian campaign. The first is financial. He revokes all the gifts of land, rights, and immunities Constantine had given to the Church and demands their repayment. Second, he changes education, forbidding Christian teachers to teach rhetoric and grammar. Third, he tries to reform paganism so it can compete with Christianity.

COMMUNITY

Love Replaced by Proto-Welfare

In a letter to Arsacius, the high priest of Galatia (362), Julian allocates grain and wine to Galatia to be used by the pagan priests, with a fifth to be expended on the poor who serve them. The remainder is to be given to strangers and beggars. As Julian notes:

> For it is disgraceful when no Jew is a beggar and the impious Galileans [Christians] support our poor in addition to their own; everyone is able to see that our coreligionists are in want of aid from us. . . . We must pay special attention to this point, and by this means effect a cure. For when it came about that the poor were neglected and overlooked by the priests, then I think the impious Galileans observe this fact and devoted themselves to philanthropy. And they have gained ascendancy in the worst of

their deeds through the credit they win for such practices.[48]

Julian tries to save paganism by making it look more Christian. Pagan priests are no longer allowed to carouse or engage in nefarious trade. Even more interesting is that Julian believes that Christian charity is the reason for its popularity. He likens it to the sweet cakes sailors would give children to entice them into slavery on their ships. His response? Government-subsidized charity.

Julian pours money and resources into pagan temples so their priests can give food to the poor. But Julian's venture is doomed to failure, because Christian charity is not a gimmick. Charity, voluntary self-devotion, brotherhood, and detachment from worldly goods are the fruit of the law of Christ and intrinsic to the Christian worldview. Christ commands his followers: "I give to you, that you love one another; even as I have loved you, that you also love one another" (John 13:34). Christian charity isn't merely something Christians do; it is who they are.

As noted earlier, pagans see Christian charity as something absurd, since it is ludicrous to care for those who are fated to be poor. Not surprisingly, once Julian dies and government support ceases, pagan "charity" stops, and so does any hope of paganism's revival.

HUMAN KNOWLEDGE
Education "Reform"

Julian also forbids the appointment of Christians to the

teaching offices of rhetoric and grammar. Here he sees how Christian teachers have colored education to reflect negatively on pagan ideals, and he wants to reverse that. Julian sees education as divine instruction, since the greatest of the Greeks' thinkers (Homer, Hesiod, Demosthenes, Herodotus, Thucydides, etc.) received their wisdom from the gods, who communicated through the muses.[49] Julian intuits the influence of the Christian worldview in education and wishes to stop it. This instinct, too, will pop up in later revolts.

THE CHURCH

Apostolic Witness Denied

Whereas Julian uses his imperial muscle against Christianity, the pagan philosopher Porphyry uses his keen intellect. Porphyry is a pagan neo-platonic philosopher, a student of the famed philosopher Plotinus, and he is best known for his fifteen-volume anti-Christian work *Against the Christians*. From the surviving fragments of this work, it appears that much of his argumentation is focused on New Testament difficulties. But Porphyry's deadliest attack is found in a different work, a lost one, titled *The Philosophy of Oracles*. The treatise is preserved in part by Augustine, who writes:

> For, as if he were about to proclaim some marvelous thing passing belief, he [Porphyry's oracle, Apollo] says, "What we are going to say will certainly take some by surprise. For the gods have declared that Christ was very

pious, and has become immortal, and that they cherish his memory: that the Christians, however, are polluted, contaminated, and involved in error. And many other such things," he says, "do the gods say against the Christians" (Augustine, City of God, XIX, 23).

Porphyry concedes the indisputable: Jesus was pious. But according to the oracle, Christ was a good pagan, who worshipped the "God, the Generator, and the King prior to all things"—a hat tip to the God of Hebrew revelation. Why, then, aren't Christians good pagans? Apollo answers: Christ's followers (i.e., the Church) distorted his memory and made him into a different figure, a myth.

Porphyry's oracle strikes at the heart of Christ's union with his Church. If the body (and its apostolic witness) has been corrupted, who is to say with certainty who and what Christ really is? If the whole Church (that is to say, the Catholic Church) was wrong, then some other revelation—from "Apollo" or any other source—could be right. Christ could be a good pagan, or a good Muslim, or anything we want to make him.

The counterattacks by Julian and Porphyry attempt to obscure the hard light of the Incarnation. For Julian, Christianity is nothing more than a philanthropical human endeavor. For Porphyry, the apostolic witness of Christ had become corrupted. What both failed to realize is that it is the truth revealed in the Incarnation that fuels Christian charity and makes the Church truly Christ's body.

9

Monasticism to Islam

If justice is giving to things what is their due
according to what they are, then one must know
what things are in order to act justly.

—ROBERT R. REILLY

From the third Christian century onward, Christian life and
charity change to meet new situations and circumstances.
Some, out of a desire to serve Christ, separate themselves
from *the world* (i.e., the allures of riches and sin), leave the cities, and live in solitude to pray and fast on the barest essentials.
Although isolated, they become quite influential. Many of
these hermits and monks receive great graces, wisdom, and
visions. They compose prayer books and work many miracles.

In addition to hermits, Christians who want to dedicate
themselves fully to the gospel, prayer, and penance form small
communities called monasteries. The meager earnings from
what the monasteries produce enable these Christians to sup-

port their own austere life as well as serve the poor and needy.

Supernatural Charity Harnesses the Power of Scale

The outpouring of charity from individual Christians is good but limited. Something more is required to meet people's needs. By pooling resources and labor, the monasteries can greatly increase their care for the poor. All that is needed is organization and leadership, which come from St. Pachomius, a former soldier, who uses his military experience to organize the monks into an effective and stable community.[50]

Monasteries grow in cities as well.

In the city, a celibate monastic had to face all the temptations Anthony had fled. Many were strong enough to stand up to them, and some were not. . . . But there were growing pains. The new city monks were too useful—too exactly what the city needed—to give up on. Just as the bishops found themselves controlling the money and influence, they needed to found institutions of Christian charity, they also found a ready and willing labor pool to staff those institutions. The monks were willing because serving the poor was what they lived for. And so it became a Christian tradition that hospitals and other charitable institutions would be staffed by religious brothers and sisters.[51]

The monks and hermits of the desert may not suffer the same temptations as those in the city, but there are other problems. Not everyone who seeks asceticism is orthodox. Arabia contains a diverse population that includes a large number of Christians, Jews, and heretical Christians whose beliefs fall somewhere between Christianity and Judaism.

Islam

Islam doesn't spring out of thin air. Rather, it appears to be an adaptation of several heretical beliefs that are in vogue in the deserts of Arabia. There are groups, for example, that claim to follow a book given by an angel.[52] Others mix Jewish and Christian practices and believe in a reoccurring *True Prophet*.[53] It is from within this Arab religious context that Muhammad comes on the scene.

GOD AND CREATION
God's Will and Nature Split

When Islam originates, it is surrounded mainly by pagan polytheists. Its adherents' desire to instill and guard the unique oneness of God leads to the denial of the Incarnation in a way far more dramatic than any of the counterattacks we have seen so far.

Unlike Arianism, Islam denies Christ's divinity outright. Muslims believe that he was born of a virgin, but they do not believe that he pre-existed his birth. The reason for this seems to be the same problem that tripped up the Arians: imagination.

The Arians could not imagine the Father's immaterial generation of the Son, so they imagined it to be like the way humans or animals generate offspring: since offspring don't exist before they are begotten, there was a time, they reasoned, when the Son did not exist.

Islam imagines the generation of the Son even more crudely than the Arians. The Quran asks, "How could he [Allah] have a son when he has no consort?" (6:100–101). The Jesus of Islam, therefore, is a holy prophet, born of the Virgin, favored by Allah, but only a man (112:1–4).

Islam is not perfectly comfortable with Christ's humanity, either. Much like the Gnostics, who recoiled at the thought of God taking on human flesh, suffering, and dying, Islam shrinks back from Christ's passion and death. According to the Quran:

> Allah's messenger—they slew him not nor crucified him, but it appeared so unto them; and lo! those who disagree concerning it are in doubt thereof; they have no knowledge thereof save pursuit of a conjecture; they slew him not for certain. But Allah took him up unto himself . . . and on the Day of Resurrection he will be a witness against them (4:157–159).[54]

The Gnostic teacher Basilides proposed an almost identical scenario:

> He thereupon appeared as a man on earth to the nations of these powers and worked wonders. And so he did not suffer, but a certain Simon of Cyrene was compelled to carry the cross for him. Through ignorance and error this Simon was

crucified, having been transformed by Christ so that he was believed to be Jesus; while Jesus himself assumed the form of Simon and, standing by, ridiculed them. For, since he was an incorporeal Power and the ingenerate Father's Mind, he was transformed as he willed, and thus he ascended to him who had sent him, deriding them, since he could not be detained and was invisible to all.[55]

Both accounts suggest divine deception, where eyewitnesses thought they had crucified Jesus, when they really hadn't.

Islam Meets the Greeks

The expansion of Islam out of the Arabian Peninsula and into Byzantium leads to the rediscovery of pagan Greek philosophy. Earlier, we saw how late second temple Judaism was confronted with Greek thought and how the result was the development of doctrine that paved the way for the incarnate Messiah and the spreading of the gospel. Greek philosophy had many errors, but its key elements are compatible with Christian revelation. Such is not the case with Islamic revelation.

Two divergent and opposing schools of Islamic thought emerge. One school is called the *Mutazilites*, whom we will call *the reason party*. On other side are the traditionalists, known as the *Asharites*, whom we will call *the irrational party*.

The reason party embraces Greek philosophy and attempts to interpret Islamic revelation to fit reason. It proposes that truth can be known not only through the Quran, but also through human reason and through the consideration of creation. The irrational party sees Greek philosophy as un-Islamic. Its members insist that Allah is so transcendent that he can be known only through Islamic revelation, not reason, nor can reason uncover any truths about God.

The divide between the two parties will not only affect the future of Islamic countries, but also ultimately culminate in a full-blown revolt against reality in Western civilization.

Each party's position raises a series of contentious questions: is the Quran eternal or created? If the Quran is not eternal—as the reason party believes—then its words are subject to interpretation, since one must first understand the historical context in which it is given. The irrational party claims that the Quran is eternal. It is God's unmediated word, so when one recites the Quran, one is literally reciting the words of God. It is not subject to interpretation. Whatever it says goes.[56]

A bigger difficulty concerns God's attributes and his will. The Greek philosophers showed that in order to exist at all, God must have several divine attributes. According to Islamic revelation, God has ninety-nine names. Some of these names describe attributes, and others describe actions. For example, one name attributed to God is *deceiver* (Arabic, *makr*) in Quran 3:54 and 8:30.[57] But this cannot be a divine attribute of God, since deception is not a perfection, but an imperfection.[58] The question arises: are these names identical to God's nature, or are they separate? The rational party says they can't be identical to his nature, since some of them imply that God can change, which is impossible. On the other hand, if they are separate from God, then that would mean that for all eternity, these things—like justice—existed alongside God, almost like separate gods, which seems to violate strict monotheism.

The rational party believes that only a few names or attributes are within God's essence, whereas the irrational party says the attributes are separate from God's essence and that Allah's will produces them.[59] This poses a problem. Take justice as an example: if justice is something God wills, then God is not just, but justice is whatever God wills it to be.

The rational party, although closer to the truth with regard to divine attributes, is still defective. As Robert Reilly notes, "The Mutazilites were the only theological school to use the term *wajib* (obligatory) in reference to God."[60] In other words, God's justice *compels* him to act justly. For the irrational party, this is blasphemous, since it imposes a law higher than God that even God has to obey!

Separating God's will from his nature effectively separates God's will from his wisdom and his wisdom from creation. If God creates however he wishes, then our ability to know God through his creation is snuffed out. Everything would depend on the unknowable God's disposition, and the only way to know that is through positive revelation.

From our earthly perspective, the unbounded (even irrational) will of God would appear virtually indistinguishable from the actions of the fickle gods of the pagan, the major difference being that there is only one God as opposed to many. The one God revealed his law, but there is nothing to guarantee that that law won't change. Indeed, God can reveal something in the Quran and later abrogate it (cause it to be no longer in effect or forgotten).[61]

The irrational party's view, therefore, restricts divine revelation to the Quran alone (and perhaps the non-Quranic revelations of Muhammad).

Avicenna, Averroes, Al-Ghazali, and Averroism

As you can see, both parties had their flaws. The Islamic polymath Avicenna (*Ibn Sīnā*) (c. 980–1037) proposed that not every person is capable of philosophical thought or grasping the fullness of truth with regard to God. Therefore, revelation is to be given to ordinary people, who are untrained in philosophy, to satisfy their need to know God. It is up to the philosophers and leaders to partake of the fullness of truth through the knowledge of first principles. In this, Avicenna mirrors Plato's *Republic*, where philosopher-kings ruled the land. Philosophical knowledge, therefore, becomes the province of the *knowing ones*, much like what we saw in Gnosticism. We will see later other areas where truth becomes compartmentalized and the exclusive province of the "experts."

The Persian theologian Al-Ghazali (1058–1111) responds with his book *The Incoherence of Philosophers*. In it, Al-Ghazali attempts to beat the philosophers at their own game and show that even on their own grounds, philosophy fails to provide demonstrative proofs more certain than revelation.[62]

The philosopher and commentator Averroes (1126–1198) responds with a line-by-line critique of Al-Ghazali titled *The Incoherence of the Incoherence*. Averroes is not a strict Mutazilite (from the rational party). He has many criticisms against their errors, along with those of the Asharites, Sufis, and *literalists*. He holds to the belief that the truths of philosophy and the truths of revelation are one and the same, but they are ordered to different people with different intellectual capacities.

Averroes's spirited defense meets with stifling opposition. The government formally rejects Averroes's writings in 1195. He is exiled to a small village outside Cordoba, Spain, where he dies a year later. His writings are banned, and his books are burned. The same is the fate of the rational party. After flourishing over the reign of several caliphs (Muslim leaders), it too is brutally suppressed by the irrational party and traditional thinkers.

HUMAN INTEGRITY AND VALUE
Free Will Denied

The question of human free will rears its head during this debate. The rational party argues that since truth exists outside Islamic revelation, and man is ordered to follow truth, man must be free to choose between good and evil. Otherwise, God rewarding the just or punishing evildoers wouldn't be proper or just, and God is just.

The irrational party opposes such talk. People, like the rest of creation, live under divine compulsion. God's will makes it so. To suggest something like free will would be tantamount to claiming there is something beyond the power of the Almighty. Seeing human freedom as somehow in competition with the sovereignty of the Creator will return during the Protestant Reformation.

The idea that man is created in the "image and likeness of God" is also foreign to Islam. Allah is master, and we are his slaves. A slave does not need to know the master's business. He needs only to hear and obey. This is quite different from the revelation of Christ to his apostles (John 15:15).

MARRIAGE AND FAMILY
Polygamy Continued

Whereas Christianity raised matrimony to a sacrament between one man and one woman for a lifetime, Islam views marriage as a contract or agreement between a man and a woman who freely consent to the marriage. Men are limited to four wives according to Islamic law, not including concubines (Quran 4:3). The marriage contract can last until divorce or death. In some branches of Shia Islam, there are temporary marriages, or *pleasure marriages*, where one is legally married for a short period of time.

THE CHURCH
Witness Denied . . . Again

If God's nature is separate from his will, then God can will things that deceive us. The Islamic account of Christ's crucifixion undermines the apostolic witness. No matter how one looks at this authentic interpretation of the surah—whether the substitute is Simon the Cyrene, Judas Iscariot, a Roman guard, or Jesus' twin—we have a divinely organized deception where God makes it appear to all (Jews, Romans, even Christ's own disciples) that someone who wasn't Jesus was Jesus. What then becomes of John's statement about what the apostles who "have heard . . . seen with our eyes . . . touched with our hands" (1 John 1:1)? Our knowledge of Christ, which comes through the witness of his body, the Church, is effectively cut off.

Like Porphyry's oracle, "Apollo," Islam holds that Christians distort the truth about Jesus being a good Muslim and an Islamic prophet who paved the way for the greatest and final prophet, Muhammad. Christians have corrupted the memory of Christ.

COMMUNITY
No Image and Likeness

If we are not made in the image and likeness of God, then our value as individuals is effectively moved from what we are to what we do. In Islam, the world is divided into those who obey and those who do not obey, the subduers and the subdued, the house of Islam and the house of war. All are not equal. The Quran institutionalizes this disparity:

Fight those who believe not in Allah nor the Last Day, nor hold forbidden that which hath been forbidden by Allah and his Messenger [Muhammad], nor acknowledge the religion of Truth, (even if they are) of the People of the Book, until they pay the jizya with willing submission, and feel themselves subdued (9:29).

The *jizya* is a heavy tax paid to maintain status as a secondary citizen. Other conditions have historically been applied to the *people of the book* in Muslim-controlled countries. For example, Christians are forbidden to erect new monasteries, churches, or sanctuaries; Christians cannot prevent any Muslim from resting in a church, day or night; Muslim guests are entitled to food and boarding for three days; children cannot be taught the Bible or publicly practice their religion or prevent their fellow Christians from converting to Islam; a Christian can never be the boss or overseer of a Muslim; etc. There is also a practice that develops in Islam known as the *blood tax* or *tribute of blood*, where Christians in occupied Muslim lands have their male children from eight to eighteen years of age taken, made to convert to Islam, and conscripted into the Islamic military. These forces are known as the Janissaries. This takes place during the reign of the Ottoman Turks, from Murad I (1362–1389) to the Sultan Mahmud II in 1826.

GOVERNMENT
Law Unhooked

The separation of God's nature from his will has dire consequences for law in general.

If justice is giving to things what is their due according

to what they are, then one must know what things are in order to act justly. Since things in the Asharite view have no nature, however, one cannot apprehend them in this way; they are only momentary assemblages of atoms.[63]

Law, therefore, becomes merely the assertion of the will of the lawgiver. If God is all-powerful and his will is essentially arbitrary in that he can will what he desires, the State likewise can will whatever it desires, provided it fits within the divine law.

HUMAN KNOWLEDGE

Science Stillborn

When pushed to its logical limits, God's unbounded will destroys the possibility of science. Since God's will does not necessarily reflect his nature, creation reflects only what an unbounded will wished to produce. A thing's nature, therefore, has no innate power. Everything is immediately caused by God. This means that the combination of two parts hydrogen and one part oxygen makes water, not because of the nature of the atoms, but because Allah wills it to be water. Allah could equally will that the combination of these same elements make a donkey or an orange.

But why does it *seem* that whenever two parts hydrogen and one part oxygen are combined, water results? The answer is that we expect it to produce water because God usually wills it to be water.[64] Science becomes, as Reilly notes, "a belief in a habit, nothing more."[65]

The laws of nature, therefore, are *not* effects produced by the overall structure and properties of things in the universe, but merely a pattern of occurrences that God habitually causes through his arbitrary will for reasons known only to himself. Therefore, God has two kinds of will: one that is regular and orderly and another that is unpredictable.

But if everything around us is a projection of God's changeable will, then the only the thing that *really* exists, despite appearances, is God.[66] Even worse, if we take this line of thought one step farther:

> If God is the only reality; then accepting the reality of the world becomes a form of polytheism—placing the real in competition with the only real. However, denying the reality of the world for this reason boomerangs back into pantheism [everything is God] by then making the world part of the only reality.[67]

The last line may sound familiar. Earlier, we learned that the pagans' "only-begotten" (*monogenes*) was an unknown god whom some equated with the cosmos.

History

The impossibility of secondary causes reduces everything to Allah's will, causing history to be understood through the prism of blessings and judgments. It is not the collision of air masses that causes a disastrous storm, but God's judgment upon the infidels. Economic successes and failures are not the product of business decisions and the economic cycle; they are God's direct, intended rewards and punishments.

Since events are linked together solely by God's will, history ceases to be a continuous interrelated story. Instead, it becomes a series of separate, distinct, and disconnected events. In Islamic countries, news events, for example, are generally not presented within their cultural and political context; rather, they are reported as a series of isolated events with no context other than a moral or religious interpretation.[68] News and history are swallowed up in a divine conspiracy.

Islam is not a monolithic religion, nor do all its believers hold to Asharitism (also known as *voluntarism* and *occasionalism*). If you were to interview the average Muslim and propose something like the voluntarism outlined above, chances are he wouldn't know what you're talking about. Nevertheless, these streams of thought have shaped how Islam presents the world, especially in areas the West has not influenced. These theological convictions are the deep cause girding the under-development of Islamic nations.

III.

ECCLESIOLOGICAL REVOLT

10

Organized Religion Saves the West

The thirteenth century deserves the
description of a great French scholar as
"the most rationalistic of all centuries."

—SIR ARNOLD LUNN

If you ever watched an old movie, you'll see behavior that
to our minds seems utterly bizarre. For example, you may
see in an old war movie a medic offering a soldier a cigarette
right before he goes into surgery. Didn't they know that
smoking was unhealthy? Yes, they did. Cigarettes had been
called *coffin nails* since the early 1880s!

Try giving a person on a gurney a cigarette before surgery today. People will think you're insane! But why is
it insane today and not forty or fifty years ago? It's the
way we are. Conventions and mainstream opinions tend
to be part of the background noise of life, and we're blind
to them unless they're presented to us to be evaluated.

But once they are, and if they happen to be rejected, an intellectual revolution begins, and things that were once accepted become unthinkable.

Christian revelation introduced new insights that began to revolutionize the West. Eventually, paganism became unthinkable. The celebration of the one un-bloody sacrifice of the Eucharist made the bloody sacrifices of paganism abhorrent. The same is true with children and women being seen as the property of men.

GOD AND CREATION
The Religious Ought

These revolutions and others could never have come about by some vague spirituality. Something concrete needed to happen. God became flesh and dwelt among us and revealed to us how things truly are. He supplied us with the religious imperative: that this is how things truly are, and they cannot be otherwise.

Culture and philosophy are incapable of producing the *religious ought*. Philosophers and philosophies come and go. Thoughts change. But it is organized religion, the historic Church, that anchors the Christian worldview to reality and through it changes the world.

The struggle is to put into practice what one knows to be true. It takes not only a religious imperative, but grace, strength, clarity, and a supportive culture. Even with these, it's easy to slip and live out of step with the truth.

History is filled with fallen Christians who did not live in accord with their beliefs. The Church will teach truth and bear witness to Christ until the end of time (Matt. 28:18–20), but that doesn't mean there won't be hypocrites. Christ never promised a perfect Church. Instead, he described it as wheat and tares. Even among the twelve apostles, there was Judas. What Jesus promised was that the Church would continue teaching "all that he had commanded" until the end of time—so that "he who hears you hears me"—and that the gates of Hades will not prevail against the Church he founded.

There is a knee-jerk reaction to organized religion in our day because of the sins and scandals caused by its members. But we do well to remember the old Latin saying, *abusus non tollit usum* (abuse does not negate use). A good thing, like organized institutions, such as the police, hospitals, schools, and others, can be abused and misused. The problem isn't these institutions *per se*, but the abuse and scandal committed within them. We do not rid ourselves of these institutions because some of the people in them are corrupt. Rather, we work to get rid of corruption. If it is true for organized services like police, hospitals, and schools, it certainly is true with organized religion.

We ought to be careful not to use our vantage point in history to condemn the past. One could look back in history and find things Christians seemingly approved or tacitly permitted that today—after the tipping point that brought about a revolution of thought and practice—we would consider abhorrent. For them, the revolution of thought was still in the future. The same is true for us today. We too live in a fog of familiarity, which one day may be dissipated when we realize how our actions do not line up with our beliefs.

Women Revered

The so-called Middle Ages are, in a real way, the flowering of many of the implications found within the Incarnation. The dignity of women is one of them. In the fullness of time, God assumed human flesh from a woman, the Blessed Virgin Mary. Mary's role in God's perfect plan of redemption restored the dignity of women by taking away the ignominy caused by Eve's role in the devil's rebellion at the beginning. Mary received the highest honor for any saint because she bore God. Moreover, it was Christ's flesh—received from Mary—that suffered and died on the cross for our sins and was resurrected and glorified.

The revolution of thought regarding women started at the Incarnation and blooms throughout early history. Women are among the earliest saints and martyrs revered by the Church, such as Ss. Perpetua, Felicity, Blandina, and Agnes, just to name a few.

Women are also heralded as great teachers. St. Macrina the elder was the grandmother of two of the great Cappadocian Fathers: Basil and Gregory of Nyssa. She was close friends with Gregory the Wonderworker (from whom we have the first recorded Marian apparition). She deserves a share of the credit for the incredible theological prose of the Cappadocians.[69]

Women feature prominently in religious life. Abbesses head the abbeys for nuns and other religious communities.

Certain women also have enormous influence in medieval culture and thought, such as St. Hildegard of Bingen (1098–1179). Hildegard is a towering intellectual figure in the twelfth century. She contributes to a wide variety of disciplines such as music, natural science, medicine, history, philosophy, art, and literature. She influences such figures as Emperor Frederick Barbarossa of Germany, the archbishop of Mainz, and King Henry II of England.

THE CHURCH

Organizing Religion

When the Roman emperor moves the capital of the empire from Rome to Constantinople in an effort to consolidate power, it fortifies the East but leaves the West vulnerable to barbarian raids and political instability. By 476, the Western Roman Empire has collapsed. A political vacuum opens up, and people undergo great suffering and injustice. The only institution left standing in the West capable of filling this vacuum is the Church.

Pope St. Gregory the Great steps into the breach. He takes on a role of temporal leadership to save the West from economic and political chaos. If the religion of the empire had been *spiritual but not religious*, Europe may not have been saved. Hence, Gregory earns the title *the Great*.

However, Gregory's heroic effort to save the West by donning the robe of temporal power exposes the Church to a new danger. Whenever the power of the State is involved, so is politics—in the bad sense of the word. Social climbers, power brokers, personal and national agendas (that can be at odds with the gospel) come with the package. Political corruption seeps into the Church, up to the highest levels.

When the successor of St. Peter, the pope, as the *servant of servants of Christ*, takes on the additional role of a temporal prince, it can be awkward, to say the least. There is no better example of this awkwardness than Pope John XII (c. 930/937–964). John XII is born Octavianus, the son of Alberic II of Spoleto, a patrician and a prominent leader within the city of Rome. After his father's death, Octavianus moves up the social ladder. Pope Agapetus II dies in November 955, and Octavianus becomes John XII.

His reign in the records reflects someone suffering from a split personality. Whenever he legislates in temporal matters, he does so under his birth name, Octavianus, but when he rules on something ecclesiastical, he uses his regnal name, John XII. Sadly, no matter what the pope is engaged in, he lives like a badly behaved prince. As the *Catholic Encyclopedia* describes him:

> The temporal and spiritual authority in Rome were thus again united in one person—a coarse, immoral man, whose life was such that the Lateran was spoken of as a brothel, and the moral corruption in Rome became the subject of general odium. War and the chase were more congenial to this pope than Church government.[70]

The reign of John XII is not how things are supposed to

go. The Church, being the body of Christ, is subject to its head, who is Jesus. This means that all members, whether they be a pope or an emperor or the poorest of the poor, are subject to a higher law. Organized religion—the Church— becomes a capping agent that limits the authority of the State. Leaders cannot rule however they wish. Emperors are children of God, members of Christ. They possess free will, and they will be judged at the end of time "according to their works" (Prov. 24:12; Sir. 11:28; 35:24; Jer. 25:14; Matt. 12:36; 16:27; Rom. 2:6; 1 Cor. 4:5; 2 Cor. 5:10; 2 Tim. 4:14; 1 Pet. 1:17). This means that when temporal rulers exercise their authority outside their proper boundaries, the lawful spiritual authority—the pope—ought to censure them.

Besides limiting government, the Church also serves the State by fostering virtuous citizens, providing education and care for the poor, encouraging communion among states, and providing moral authority and lending legitimacy to the ruling sovereign. Church and State mutually support each other. At least, that's how it is supposed to be.

Unfortunately, it is during the time of John XII— paradoxically, when rational argument is held at a premium—that the worst of power politics takes place. What happens when a ruler, who is a Catholic only in name, rules unjustly? Does he receive correction by the pope and mend his ways, or will he turn his people against the pope? It is during this time that marginally Catholic sovereigns choose the latter.

Monasteries to Hospitals

As monasteries grow and use the economics of scale to support the religious motto *ora et labora* (prayer and work), Christian doctors come and help the monasteries offer further care for the poor. Eventually, religious open up houses dedicated to serving the sick. These houses grow and develop into religious-run hospitals. Charitable gifts increase and need to be managed on a larger scale, with bishops often coordinating and allocating funds to areas in need.

The Albigensian Crusade

The Gnosticism that St. Irenaeus of Lyons crushed in the third century raises its ugly head during the twelfth and thirteenth centuries in Albi, France. A new dualistic group becomes known as the *Albigensians* or *Cathari* (the pure). The Albigensians believe in two creator gods or *principles*, one good and the other evil. Like what the Gnostics believed, the good god created spiritual things and the evil god material things. The Albigensians' radical anti-material bent moves them to observe strict continence, both inside and outside marriage, since the carnal act could produce children, meaning more souls trapped in material bodies. They also forbid taking oaths, which is an integral part of feudal society. Since governments govern the material world, they think loyalty to a government means being under the dominion of the evil god. Therefore, they consider themselves exempt from obeying earthly rulers, which essentially places them in rebellion against authorities.

Were this heresy allowed to spread throughout Europe, the results would be catastrophic. It needs to be stopped. The response comes from temporal rulers and from the Church.

First, there is the appeal to reason and conversion. Preachers are sent to the Albigensians to combat their errors, but they don't accomplish much. When the sect becomes more violent, Pope Innocent III (1160–1216) calls a crusade to suppress them, since their beliefs are spreading to other locations and becoming a threat to all of Europe.

The Albigensian Crusade is not merely a religious squabble. It is civilization battling an intellectual and seditious enemy. Catholicism, reason, and civilization win a definitive victory against the insanity embraced by the Albigensians. However, this will prove to be one of the last such victories.

HUMAN KNOWLEDGE
Modern Science Born

Organized religion also saves Western civilization during the barbarian raids. Monasteries are usually founded on donated land, which is less than ideal. Often, these lands are swamp-infested areas that no one wishes to live on. The monks, out of necessity, develop techniques and technology to transform swampland into good, fertile soil. The innovations shared among monasteries and supported by the Church turn the so-called *Dark Ages* into a mini-Industrial Revolution.

Moreover, organized religion saves and preserves the knowledge and wisdom of the past. No monastery is alone; rather, they network and share information, increasing the survivability of the whole. They also prioritize copying and preserving knowledge. In rooms called *scriptoria*, monks dedicate untold hours to copying ancient works.

Since Christianity sees all that is true, just, beautiful, and good as coming in some way from God, the monks' labors are not restricted to Christian works. They copy everything from pagan philosophy to even Greek erotic poetry. Manuscripts are passed from monastery to monastery, duplicating and preserving the same works. This built-in redundancy enables these works to survive so that if one monastery is destroyed, the loss is minimized by the fact that much of its library was duplicated elsewhere. Once the barbarians are converted, the raids cease, and ancient knowledge is preserved in the West.

Science

Organized religion supplies the religious imperative and realistic worldview needed to ignite scientific investigation as a self-sustaining enterprise. The sacred texts produced during the *Greek miracle*, including Sirach, Wisdom, and 2 Maccabees, made unique contributions to the foundations of modern science. In 2 Maccabees, for example, it is explicitly affirmed that God created everything from nothing (*ex nihilo*). The books of Wisdom and Sirach anchored belief in a universe that is intelligible and knowable in its totality. The most important and frequently quoted text from this period is Wisdom 11:20, which links abstractions with creation when it states of God, "But thou hast arranged all things by measure and number and weight" (Wis. 11:20).

Numbers, measure, and weight are not physical objects, but intellectual objects. You can't go to the store and buy a *two* or trip over a *three* while hiking. But when we see a pair of stones, our minds can understand them to have a *two-ness*.

Measure and weight are comparative statements. A *comparison* doesn't exist as a thing, but it is something our minds recognize and use. The same is true with weight.

Wisdom 11:20 teaches with the certainty of inspired revelation that our minds know the language in which the nature of all things—visible and invisible—are made. Physical things, therefore, can be known and understood through math, measurement, comparisons, and so on.

Greek philosophers recognized the link between nature and abstractions. But the philosophy of Pythagoras was just that—the philosophy of Pythagoras. People were free to accept it or reject it. What the Church possesses that these other philosophies lacked is the religious imperative—these things *must* be so and cannot be otherwise. Nature doesn't just *seem* to be comprehensible by abstraction; it *is* disposed to be understood in this way. The confidence this imperative instills enables the Christian West to investigate nature with the expectation that all of it is intelligible.

As the physicist and theologian Stanley Jaki points out in several of his works, the innate genius of human intelligence is present in every age and in every nation. Each contributes to the advancement of human knowledge. All cultures, from the East (Chinese, Indian) to the West (Babylonian, Greek, Muslim, etc.), contribute something unique to this venture. But what these cultures lack is a worldview that reflects reality. Put another way, they supply the ingredients necessary to produce modern science, but they don't have the recipe necessary to put all the different elements together. It is the Church as an institution that supplies the recipe and the religious *ought* that gives birth to modern science.

Organized religion kicks off the scientific revolution when the Fourth Lateran Council (1215) asserts as dogma (something necessary to believe as a Christian) that God created all things at once out of nothing.[71] It is this definition and the Condemnations of 1277—as we shall soon see—that impel Jean Buridan (1300–1358) to create the first scientific revolution of thought. As Stacy Trasancos notes:

> Buridan was not a theologian, but a man with a brilliant scientific mind. While confident in his faith to guide his thinking and lay boundaries for reality, he was most interested in explaining natural phenomenon [*sic*], particularly the motion of objects, and, even more particularly the beginning of all motion. His assent of faith to the tenets of the Christian creed guided him to assert the most critical breakthrough in the history of science, the idea of inertial motion and *impetus*.[72]

Buridan's impetus leads to the modern idea of inertia and clears the way for Newton's first law of motion. The rest is history. It is the religious imperative that supplies the motivating force to investigate nature because it is viewed as another way to see and to adore God's wisdom, which nature reflects.

Cathedral Schools to University System

Organized religion also brings about what will become the modern university. Since the Church is a single unified body that expanded over a large geographical area and holds natural philosophy, the sciences, and revelation at a premium, it is able to create and coordinate a system of education that eventually becomes modern institutes of higher learning. Like the formation of modern science, this system is unique to Christendom.[73]

This endeavor is a partnership between the Church and the State to provide educated leaders. These schools have textbooks, curricula, and a program of studies that last for a particular period. They issue various levels of degrees, including a master's degree that enables its bearers to teach. Nearly all universities obtain a charter for accreditation. As historian Thomas Wood explains:

Some 81 universities had been established by the time of the Reformation. Of these 33 possessed a papal charter, 15 a royal or imperial one, 20 possessed both, and 13 had none. In addition, it was the accepted view that a

university could not award degrees without the approba-
tion of pope, king, or emperor. . . . The pope (in fact)
and the emperor (in theory) possessed authority over all
of Christendom, and for this reason it was to them that
a university typically had to turn for the right to issue
degrees. Equipped with the approval of one or the other
of these universal figures, the university's degrees would
be respected throughout all of Christendom.[74]

Like the monastic system, whose members share technology and information, the Church's catholicity enables it to
set up an international exchange of ideas, education, and
accreditation, so that a discovery or theory in one country
can be relayed to other universities throughout Europe for
further discussion and development. This system becomes
the engine for scientific and technological advancements.

The True Age of Reason

The twelfth and thirteenth centuries in many ways should
be called the true "age of reason." In this age, philosophy, natural philosophy, theology, Scripture, and authority
become synthesized in a refreshing and insightful way. This
synthesis, springing from Christian revelation and practice,
begins to produce abundant intellectual and aesthetic fruit.

The *Age of Reason* is usually applied to the so-called
Enlightenment, as if that movement were the apex of reason
and rational thought, but as Sir Arnold Lunn notes, this title
is more justly given to the thirteenth century.

Those who accept with uncritical satisfaction the popular and flattering contrast between the credulous medieval and the hard headed and rational Victorian, fail to realize the Victorian rationalism was a product of the flight from reason, whereas the thirteenth century deserves the description of a great French scholar as "the most rationalistic of all centuries." . . . Why, then, does this great synthesis possess so narrow and so eclectic an appeal?[75]

Lunn answers:

The modern believer has exchanged the austere mental climate of the thirteenth century, a climate warmed only by the cold light of reason, for the more temperate zone of intuition and personal experience.[76]

In the next chapter, we will see the first shots fired in Lunn's "revolt against reason" with the battle between Ludwig of Bavaria and Pope John XXII.

11

Marsilius of Padua and William of Ockham

God's will alone determines what is good
and evil, and he is not even bound by his own
previous determinations.

—MICHAEL ALLEN GILLESPIE

In 1313, the holy Roman emperor, Henry VII, dies, leaving the imperial throne vacant. Germany splits into three dynastic factions, the Wittelsbach (Bavaria), the Habsburg (Austria), and the Luxembourg (Bohemia). The Wittelsbach and Luxembourg houses ally against the Habsburg faction, and in October of that year, two emperors are elected. The Wittelsbachs and Habsburgs elect Ludwig the Bavarian (1282–1347), and the Luxembourgs elect Frederick the Fair (1289–1330). Both parties almost immediately go to war. Since these elections take place during a papal vacancy (Pope Clement V had died in the spring of the same year), there is no way to settle the matter until a new pope is elected. That pope is Pope John XXII (r. 1316–1334). The new pope issues a bull, *Si fratum* (1317), that calls for both Ludwig and Frederick I to abdicate within three months or face excommunication. Both ignore the pope's bull. Ludwig eventually subdues Fredrick I in 1322, imprisons him for three years, and releases him after he signs a document that makes him essentially an honorific emperor. This is the opening shot in a long-running and destructive battle between Ludwig and John XXII.

Ludwig counters the pope's excommunication (1324) with armies and argument. With regard to the latter, Ludwig offers protection to anti-papal intellectuals and enlists them to undermine the authority of the Church and especially the papacy. Two such intellectuals are Marsilius of Padua (1275–1342) and William of Ockham (1287–1347). To understand these two, we must first look at the controversies from which they came.

GOD AND CREATION
Truth and God Divided

The expansion of Islam brought new Greek philosophical works to the Latin West, along with Islamic commentaries on them. The reception of these texts, and especially Aristotelian philosophy, was so positive that many teachers and students began to embrace uncritically everything Aristotle taught. True, Aristotle was a great philosopher, but he made some serious errors (pantheism, the uncreated eternal cosmos, all humans share one intellect, etc.).[77] The confusion was compounded by Islamic commentators, such as Averroes, who followed Aristotle in some of these errors.

Double Truth

One way academics try to avoid the contradiction of embracing both Aristotle and the Faith is to adopt something called *double truth* (also known as *hard Averroism*). Double truth separates faith and reason into exclusive spheres of knowledge so that a person can affirm as true something taught in one sphere and affirm its contradiction in another.

St. Thomas Aquinas's criticism of Siger Brabant in this regard is instructive:

> It is yet more wonderful, indeed worthy of indignation, that anyone professing himself to be a Christian should presume to speak so irreverently of the Christian faith as to say that, "The Latins do not accept this as a principle," namely, that there is only one intellect, "perhaps because their law is contrary to it." . . . Afterward he said, "This is the reason why Catholics seem to hold their position," where the judgment of the faith is called a position! . . . Even more serious is this subsequent remark: "Through reason I conclude necessarily that intellect is numerically one, *but I firmly hold the opposite by faith*." Therefore, he thinks faith is of things whose contrary can be necessarily concluded; since the only thing that can be necessarily concluded is a necessary truth whose opposite is false and impossible.[78]

By separating faith and reason into two mutually exclusive and distinct areas of knowledge, the Latin Averroists reduce the faith to a mere position, not at all different from a philosophy. Instead of dividing reality into two spheres, scholars need to apply the religious imperatives of revelation to Aristotle's thought so as to purify it and allow it to reach new heights. In other words, Aristotle's thought needs to be baptized.

The University of Paris

The baptism begins in 1210 through a series of condemnations of various propositions propounded by individuals in the arts faculty at the University of Paris.[79] It culminates in Bishop Stephen Tempier's condemnation in 1277 of 219 propositions, which are directed not only to errors in Aristotle, but also to various topics such as necromancy, fortune-telling, invocation of devils, and curses.[80]

Bishop Tempier begins his condemnations by speaking against double truth.

> For they say that these things are true according to philosophy but not according to the Catholic faith, as if there were two contrary truths and as if the truth of Sacred Scripture were contradicted by the truth in the sayings of the accursed pagans.[81]

The impact of the condemnations is limited, but although they don't stop Latin Averroists, they do weaken the grip Aristotle had as the last word in philosophy.

Marsilius of Padua

One Latin Averroist who escapes the condemnations is Marsilius of Padua (1275–1342), who serves as rector at the University of Paris in 1313. Marsilius and John of Jandun (1280–1328) write *Defensor Pacis* (1324), which takes Averroes's hierarchy of knowers—the common man (who understands primarily through imagination), the philosopher (who learns partly through philosophy), and the philosopher-ruler (who desires to learn through reason alone)—and applies it to the political order.

Since the philosopher-ruler operates on reason alone, *Defensor Pacis* begins by laying out a purely rationalistic politic. The Second Discourse then appeals to revelation to "confirm" what had already been established by reason. As Hahn and Wiker note:

> The salient point of this procedure is that it permits the establishment of the central doctrines of the political philosophy in complete disregard of the supernatural order. Hence, when revelation is invoked . . . a complete rational, non-supernatural political system lies already at hand, and the texts of Scripture can be so selected and interpreted as to support that system.[82]

Once the authors of *Defensor Pacis* become known and are condemned as heretics, they flee to the protection of Ludwig of Bavaria, who welcomes them with open arms. After all, their work provides a philosophical framework that undermines the authority of John XXII, if not the Church as a whole.

William of Ockham

William of Ockham (whom we will simply call Ockham) is also a Latin Averroist, but his story is a bit different. Ockham is a member of the Franciscan order, known for its strict adherence to poverty. The Franciscans grew numerous after their founder's death, and the question arises whether the Franciscans need to relax their strict rules to accommodate this growth. A split eventually erupts between the *spirituals*, who wish to adhere to St. Francis's original rule, and the *conventionals*, who wish to relax it.

Pope Celestine V, in 1294, permits the spirituals to adopt the strict rule of Francis. However, he reigns for only six months, and his successor, Boniface VIII, withdraws this approval and condemns the spirituals. With the ascension of John XXII to the papal throne, the head of the spirituals is summoned to the papal court in Avignon to stand trial.

William of Ockham is also summoned to Avignon to defend himself against accusations of heresy. While there, the head of Ockham's order asks him to defend the spirituals' position in their dispute with the pope over *apostolic poverty*. The dispute is not a mere squabble about living out the gospel; at its core, it is a dispute over the nature of God.

The Poverty Dispute turned upon a decisive theological distinction. The Franciscan order believed that Christ had renounced his kingdom and world dominion and that they should imitate him by taking a vow of poverty. . . . Pope John XXII argued that Christ could not have renounced his kingdom because it would contradict what was ordained by God. The Franciscans replied that while God would not do this by his ordained power, he could do so by his absolute power, that is, God was not bound by his past actions. . . . The Poverty Dispute in this sense was a concrete form of the debate over the relationship between divine will and reason . . . arguing that if God is free and sovereign, he can predestine whomever he chooses. Hence, the pope was a heretic.[83]

Ockham's propositions are censured but not condemned—yet. In 1328, Ockham, like Marsilius of Padua, flees Avignon to Ludwig of Bavaria. Under Ludwig's protection, he and Marsilius circulate their views that delegitimize the papacy and place imperial rule above that of the Church.

God's Unconstrained Will

Like the irrational party (the Asharites) in Islam, according to the spirituals, God's will is separated from his nature. God wills the good not because he is goodness itself, but rather because he decided to will it at that moment. Later, God could call the same thing evil. This is precisely what was argued in the Poverty Dispute. The spirituals argued that God could will that property is a good in the Old

Testament, but in the New Testament, he chose to will the opposite. Ockham's thought has striking implications:

> There is no immutable law or reason. Every order is simply the result of God's absolute will and can be disrupted or reconstituted at any moment. Indeed, Ockham even maintains that God can change the past if he so desires.[84]

According to this view, reality is not a coherent whole, like a fabric comprising individual threads woven into a tapestry. Reality is more like a computer screen made up of individual pixels. Each pixel is isolated, disconnected, and separate from the others and can change to produce different pictures on the screen.

Therefore, God's establishment of creatures "according to their kind" is turned into a kind of fiction. Universals (like animality and triangularity) are nothing more than names (Latin, *nomina*) we assign to things for the purpose of comprehending the incomprehensible multitude of radically individual things. For Ockham, "divine omnipotence, properly speaking, thus entails radical individualism."[85] By rejecting the God of reason and replacing him with a god of will, Ockham—like the Asharites—essentially rules out the possibility of knowing God through the things he has made.

Divine Deception

There is a deeper and more insidious implication to Ockham's view. It opens the possibility that God can deceive us:

Divine omnipotence, however, raises a fundamental epistemological problem, since it opens up the possibility of divine deception. . . . For Ockham, the idea of divine omnipotence thus means that human beings can never be certain that any of the impressions they have correspond to an actual object.[86]

Heaven and earth separated by God's unbounded will make it impossible for us to know what anything truly is. Ockham, however, stops short of this radical conclusion:

Ockham believes that God acts in such a manner only rarely, but this does not remove the epistemological problem, for even if he were never to act in such a manner, it would be sufficient to undermine the certainty of all knowledge.[87]

We saw the same kind of response from the irrational party in Islam. God habitually wills things in a certain way. But once you allow even the possibility that God could will otherwise, you've undermined all certain knowledge and opened up the possibility of divine deception. We saw the same implications in earlier revolts, from the serpent's lie in the garden to Gnosticism to the traditionalists in Islam. Ockhamism (also known as *nominalism*) separates God's wisdom from his will and God from creation, and it dissolves our ability to know what is real.

Revelation Alone

If God cannot be known through the things he has made, the only way to know the unbounded will of God is through revelation. The outward appearance of things becomes meaningless.

The radical implications of this can be seen with regard to the sacraments. The sacraments are outward visible signs of an interior invisible reality. Under nominalism, the sacraments lose their inherent meaning and coherence, since God could will that a person be "baptized" with sand or that candles be transubstantiated. The connection between visible outward signs and the invisible reality they point to is broken. What is left? Ultimately, our union with God is reduced to faith alone.[88]

God's arbitrary absolute will has the same disastrous consequences for our redemption.

> God could have saved by any means. . . . Christ could have been incarnate as a stone, a block of wood, or even an ass, or more importantly God could justify sinners directly without creating any specific habit in the individual.[89]

Christ's humanity isn't denied, but it is seen as arbitrary. When Ockham's nominalism is pushed to its logical conclusion, there can be no real (ontological) union with Christ, since Christ's humanity is merely something God willed with no rhyme or reason. He could have assumed a nature that is radically different from our own. And if Christ's humanity is arbitrary, then the apostolic witness of what was seen, heard, and touched is meaningless. Christ's body—the Church—is nothing more than a name we give to a collection of similar individuals.

The Moral Law

The natural law and the moral law fare no better under Ockham's nominalism:

> The moral law is in this sense radically subordinated to divine choice and completely beyond the capacity of human reason to deduce or explain. . . . God is indifferent to what he chooses and the moral law is good not in itself but only because he wills it. Moreover, there is no limits set upon what God can demand. He can even command that we hate him. Whatever his commandments may be, they are by definition good and binding. God's will alone determines what is good and evil, and he is not even bound by his own previous determinations.[90]

Lastly, nominalism ushers in a new form of radical individualism that mirrors the nominalist god.[91]

For Ockham, individual human beings have no natural end, and there is no natural law such as Aquinas had imagined to govern human actions. Man, like God is free . . . opening up this realm of freedom not merely by rejecting the scholastic notion of final causes, but also by rejecting the application of efficient causality to men. For Ockham, man in principle is thus free from nature itself.[92]

The outworking of nominalism will ultimately come to full bloom in the twenty-first century with the insanity of feminism, bodily autonomy, abortion, and gender identity.

The god of Ockham is the antithesis of Christ, Emmanuel, God with us. The Incarnation proposes that God's wisdom permeates all and that his love binds us as one body. The nominalist god, by contrast, is unknowable apart from what he has revealed through positive revelation. He is a god shrouded in darkness, whose will is, from our perspective, fickle and arbitrary, much like the gods and goddesses in pagan myths.

MARRIAGE AND FAMILY
Temporal Control

Just as individuals mirror the nominalist god with regard to the moral law, so does the State. This point is made clear with regard to the sacrament of matrimony:

> In his controversial writings William of Ockham appears as the advocate of secular absolutism. He denies the right of the popes to exercise temporal power, or to interfere in any way whatever in the affairs of the empire. He even went so far as to advocate the validity of the adulterous marriage of Louis's son, on the grounds of political expediency, and the absolute power of the State in such matters.[93]

When Ludwig of Bavaria is unable to obtain a Catholic bishop's co-operation to nullify his son's marriage to Margaret, the heiress of Tyrol:

> Marsilius and William of Ockham, came to his aid, by writing treatises in which it was maintained that the jurisdiction in such cases belonged, not to the Church, but to the temporal sovereign; that had belonged to the heathen emperors, and therefore much more must it be the right of the Christian emperor; that, while it is for bishops and theologians to decide whether certain defects in one of the parties would justify to the secular judge; that "it is for the human lawgiver to order that to be done which is established by divine law."[94]

The course advocated by Marsilius and Ockham is a step back to paganism, where the sovereign reigns over all things. Bishops and theologians can investigate the case, but ultimately, the decision is left to the temporal ruler. In this case, Ludwig himself annuls his son's marriage.

THE CHURCH
Dulling the Spiritual Sword

Ludwig not only strikes at Christianity intellectually, but also uses force, entering Rome on January 11, 1328 and crowning himself emperor, since the pope had refused to crown him. On April 18, Ludwig issues a decree deposing the pope on the grounds of heresy and considers appointing an antipope to take his place.

The pope fights back against Ludwig with the spiritual sword. He issues a series of excommunications extending down to kindred with Ludwig to the fourth degree. He also places whole countries under the interdict. As Karl Adams explains:

> Germany alone was under interdict for twenty years, which means that no public religious service could be held, no sacrament could be publicly administered, no bell could sound. The more often these ecclesiastical penalties were imposed, the blunter grew the spiritual sword. Inevitably the religion and morality of the people suffered serious damage, their sense of the Church was weakened, their sympathies were alienated from Christ's vicar.[95]

The pope also fills all the vacant sees and offices in Germany with his supporters, which fosters more alienation between the German people and the Church.[96]

John XXII dies in 1334. In the summer of 1346, Charles IV, a member of the house of Luxembourg, is elected king of the Romans with the support of John's successor, Pope Clement VI. Civil war is avoided when Ludwig dies of a stroke while bear-hunting in October 1347.

COMMUNITY

Blurring Temporal and Spiritual

Since the Church has taken on temporal offices of great importance, and such offices are often endowed with great wealth, wealth becomes a distraction from living a Christlike life. Reform is needed, but who will bring it about? Many times, the calls for reforming the Church come from Gnostic-like heretics (who look upon the possession of any material things as evil) or political opportunists who wish to strip the Church of both her spiritual and her temporal authority, such as Marsilius of Padua and William of Ockham. Ultimately, it is up to the bishops of the Church or a council to take the matter in hand. Many prelates and religious promote reform, but little is done to stop the corruption.

HUMAN KNOWLEDGE
The Modern Way

Ludwig's intellectual scorched-earth tactics reverberate long after his death. It's clear from the reaction to Ockham's philosophy and theology that the Church understands their destructiveness. Measures are taken—such as universities requiring their teachers to take oaths against teaching Ockhamism—to prevent their spread. But for a variety of reasons too complex to explain here, Ockham's teaching proliferates anyway. Nominalism seems fresh, innovative, and modern. Indeed, it becomes known as the *via moderna* (the modern way) as opposed to the *via antiqua* (the ancient way) that followed Thomas Aquinas and the scholastics. By the time of the Protestant Revolt, nominalism has become the predominant school of thought in the universities.

12

The Protestant Revolution

Thus a Christian man is righteous and a sinner

at the same time, holy and profane,

an enemy of God and a child of God.

—MARTIN LUTHER

Christ's humanity both manifested and veiled his divinity. His divinity was manifested through his words, deeds, and miracles, yet Jesus didn't look different from anyone else. He still got dirty, had the same bodily functions, was injured, suffered, and died.

A similar phenomenon can be seen in his body, the Church. It manifests its union with Christ through its teachings, its love, its miracles, its sacraments, and its saints. At the same time, this union is obscured by the sinfulness, foolishness, and infidelity of its members.

It is in the centuries leading up to the Protestant revolt that the divine element of the Church is most obscured, especially by the scandalous and shockingly sinful behavior of some who sit in the chair of St. Peter. As Karl Adams notes:

> The most sober ecclesiastical historians agree that the reigns of the popes from Sixtus IV [1471–1484] to Leo X [1513–1521] "represent from the religious and ecclesiastical point of view, the lowest level of the papacy since the tenth and eleventh centuries."[97]

Most of the bishops who serve under these popes are more worldly than godly. The clergy, on the other hand, suffer from having little money and little education. Although the laity are disgruntled by the rich and powerful prelates, clerical abuses, and the problems associated with issues concerning the Church's land ownership, laypeople nevertheless reach new heights in terms of their rich devotion to the Faith.

We shouldn't underestimate the scandalous behavior of Church leaders during this period, but we also should not exaggerate it. There are many examples of holy and sincere Christian leadership as well:

> It was the age of the three Catherines, of Siena, Bologna and Genoa; the age when St. Bridget scourged the abuses of the Avignon Curia with the flames of her wrath, when Thomas à Kempis [1379–1471] wrote his immortal Imitation of Christ. . . . As early as 1245 at the Council of Lyons, Pope Innocent IV [1243–1254] had called the sins of the higher and lower clergy one of the five wounds in

the body of the Church, and at the Second Council of Lyons in 1274 Pope Gregory X [1271–1276] declared that the wickedness of many prelates was the cause of the ruin of the whole world.[98]

It is during this period of reform that our next revolt begins—where people, under the guise of reform, attempt to strip Christianity of its incarnational essense without denying the Incarnation itself.

Martin Luther

Martin Luther (1483–1546) is the son of a peasant miner. His father hopes young Martin will become a lawyer, but his direction changes at Erfurt, where he decides to study philosophy and religion. Erfurt is considered a *via moderna* stronghold. It is here that Luther encounters nominalism and, to a lesser extent, scholasticism. But it is ultimately a pilgrimage to Rome, with all its worldliness and corruption, that sets him in motion.

This being said, it is important to note that the "abuses in the Church were not the real *cause* but only the *occasion* of the Reformation."[99] Luther is not concerned with reforming the morals of the clergy; his concern is doctrine. As Hahn and Wiker summarize it:

In his [Luther's] later words, "Life is as evil among us as among the papists, thus we do not argue about life but about doctrine. Whereas Wycliff and Hus attacked the immoral lifestyle of the papacy, I challenge primarily its doctrine." Or to put it in a more startling way, even if the ecclesiastical hierarchy had been exhibiting exemplary holiness at the time, Luther would, it seems, have attacked its doctrine as fundamentally flawed.[100]

On October 31, 1517, Luther publishes his Ninety-Five Theses that contest the efficacy of indulgences, among other items. In 1521, at the Diet of Worms (a meeting of the imperial deliberative body), Pope Leo X and the Holy Roman Emperor, Charles V, demand that Luther renounce all of his writings. In response, Luther says, reputedly, "Here I stand. I can do no other." The Holy Roman Emperor excommunicates him and condemns him as an outlaw. Like Ockham before him, Luther escapes into the protection of a patron, the elector of Saxony, Fredrick III.

GOD AND CREATION
Championing the Nominalist Divide

Luther is a nominalist, but not a thoroughgoing one.[101] In 1520, he writes:

> I demand arguments not authorities. That is why I contradict even my own school of Ockhamists, which I have absorbed completely.[102]

Although Luther criticizes some teachings of nominalists like Ockham, Gabriel Biel, and Peter of Ailly, he nevertheless holds to the same nominalist distinction between God's unbounded absolute will and his habitual ordained will.[103]

Scripture Alone

It's not surprising that Luther's nominalism, as with the Islamic Asharites before him, leads to restricting our knowledge of God to positive revelation alone. This is the first step toward displacing the perpetual witness of Christ's visible body, the Church, as the norm through which we have fellowship with God (1 John 1:1–2) with the Bible. No longer do we hear Christ by hearing the apostolic Church; we are to hear Christ solely through inspired Scripture.

HUMAN INTEGRITY AND VALUE
Faith Alone and the Body-Soul Dichotomy

Luther's view of God also affects his view of how sinners are made acceptable to God in justification:

> The Church's classical doctrine of grace, presents grace as a movement of divine love, entering into the penitent soul and delivering it from the bonds of its fallen nature. In contrast with this, grace in Ockhamism remains strictly transcendent. Justification consists solely in a *relatio externa*, a new relationship of mercy between man and God established by God's love, by means of which all man's religious and moral acts, though remaining in themselves human and natural, are accounted as salvific acts in the eyes of the merciful God. . . . Human activity only becomes salvific

by God's recognition of it, by his act of acceptance. But this recognition and validation does not in any way affect man's spiritual powers. It remains completely outside him and is simply seen and assented to by faith.[104]

According to nominalism, God gives us the Law to follow and subsequently approves whatever moral acts we do, as he pleases—a view that comes close to denying the doctrine of original sin. Luther's struggle to earn salvation, the nominalist way, pushes him to the point of hating God. His crisis is alleviated by reading Romans 3:28: "For we hold that a man is justified by faith apart from works of law." The law, Luther thinks, is given to drive us to our knees in despair, knowing we can never be righteous in the sight of God and that when we place our faith in Christ, he declares or treats us as if we were righteous.

Catholicism teaches, however, that the just God wills justly. Therefore, when God calls an individual *just*, the individual is changed and becomes just because God's Word is a creative Word (Rom. 5:18–19; 1 John 3:1). Being united to Christ in justification, as a branch to a vine, we bear good fruit—that is, good works that are pleasing to God (John 15:1–6; 1 John 3:7)—because it is God who produces these good works that are pleasing to him (1 Cor. 15:10; Eph. 3:8–10; Phil. 2:12–13).

Luther considers justification, as the nominalists do, as completely external to us: God declares us righteous even though we remain unrighteous in ourselves. Unlike Ockham, however, Luther asserts that man is incapable of

doing any truly good work, since Adam's sin utterly corrupted our nature.

By reducing justification to faith alone, we—as soul-body
composites—are treated in a dichotomous way. Fidelity to
God is split into two opposing camps: faith alone (i.e., trust
in God's promises) is what pleases God and justifies us, as
opposed to anything we do. God accepts the soul's assent of
faith. As for our bodily acts of obedience, God either ignores
them or takes offense at them.

Luther's Contrary Truths

Since justification is an external decree of God, Luther
describes those justified as being simultaneously "just and
sinner" (*simul justus et peccator*). As Luther writes in his *Lectures on Galatians* (1535):

> Thus a Christian man is righteous and a sinner at the same
> time, holy and profane, an enemy of God and a child of
> God. None of the sophists will admit this paradox, because
> they do not understand the true meaning of justification.[105]

In this view of justification, God is said to treat us *as if
we were* righteous and worthy of salvation even though in
reality, we are unchanged (profane, sinful, damnable). The
Church teaches something very different: a real transformation occurs in justification, where the sinner ceases to
be a profane enemy of God and, being grafted to the New
Adam, becomes holy and righteous.

Luther's view vaguely parallels the dualism we saw earlier with the Gnostics, whose salvation consisted of the soul discarding the materiality of the body by obtaining secret knowledge.

Free Will

Where Ockham believed that man had a bestowed freedom, Luther denies free will outright, famously likening it to a beast of burden:

> If God rides it, it goes where God wills. . . . If Satan rides it, it wills and goes where Satan wills; nor can it choose to run to either of the two riders or to seek him out, but the riders themselves contend for the possession and control of it.[106]

We saw a similar error with the Islamic irrational party, who claimed that everything except God acts under compulsion.

MARRIAGE AND FAMILY

Monogamy and Polygamy

Earlier, Ockham and Marsilius approved of their patron and protector nullifying the marriage of his son due to "extenuating circumstances." Luther and Philip Melanchthon (1497–1560) will suggest ceding even greater power over marriage to the State for political expediency.

When King Henry VIII of England (1491–1547) desires to divorce his lawful wife, Catherine of Aragon

(1485–1536), Luther counsels that "better were it for her to allow the king to wed another queen, after the example of the patriarchs, who, in the ages previous to the law, had many wives."[107] He believes that monogamous marriage is a time-honored tradition but that there is no outright prohibition in Scripture against taking more than one wife. Melanchthon, a theologian who collaborates with Luther, likewise detests polygamy but feels that the sovereigns can—out of political expediency—be permitted to have more than one wife.[108]

Luther and Melanchthon are only spectators at Henry VIII's divorce. However, later, the issue of bigamous marriage will compel them to speak directly to the issue.

> In 1539, the landgrave [Philip of Hess] resolved to take as an additional wife, besides Christina the daughter of George of Saxony, who had now grown distasteful to him, the more youthful Margaret von der Sale. From Luther Margaret's mother desired a favorable pronouncement, in order to be able with a good conscience to give her consent to her daughter's wedding.[109]

The response was that scandal was the only impediment for Phillip taking a second wife:

> And, as your Serene Highness has determined to take another wife, we consider that this should be kept secret, no less than the dispensation, viz. that your Serene Highness

and the lady in question, and a few other trustworthy persons, should be apprised of your Highness's conscience and state of mind in the way of confession.[110]

The letter is signed by Luther, Melanchthon, and fellow German Protestant reformer Martin Bucer. Following Ockham's teaching, the temporal rulers can grant themselves annulments, and even a dispensation to have two wives, if the circumstances are considered grave enough. The public should be told a "holy lie" to avoid scandal.

The "For Me" Faith

Luther's loose view regarding the exclusive one-flesh union of marriage and the separation of the soul (faith) and body (works) in justification has serious ramifications for Christ's one-flesh union with his Church. Ephesians 5:29–32 likens this union to the one-flesh union of a marriage, with the husband nurturing the wife's body as his own.

Luther affirms this one-flesh unity, but he spiritualizes it and divides it into his body/soul, exterior/interior, and faith/works dichotomies. Luther writes:

Just as a bridegroom possesses all that is his bride's and she all that is his—for the two have all things in common because they are one flesh [Gen. 2:24]—so Christ and the church are *one spirit* [Eph. 5:29–32].[111]

Notice how Luther switches from the one-flesh union of Adam and Eve in Genesis 2:24 to a "one spirit" union of Christ with his Church. This point is made clearer a little later in the same work:

The third incomparable benefit of faith is that *it unites the soul with Christ as a bride is united with her bridegroom.* By this mystery, as the apostle teaches, Christ *and the soul* become one flesh [Eph. 5:31–32].[112]

Although Luther's words fit perfectly with his views of faith alone and all the dichotomies that go with it, his take mangles Paul's teaching beyond recognition. Paul did not say, "Christ and *the soul* become one flesh." He couldn't have. The soul is immaterial; there is no flesh to unite!

Luther's views, by the way, plant the seeds for the modern rationale for so-called *same-sex marriage*—claiming that love (a faculty of the soul) is the only essential component to marriage, not a one-flesh union or its being ordered toward the propagation of children.

Reflexive Faith

Before Luther, faith could be understood as viewing Christ through the eyes of his bride, the Church. Since there is one Lord (and one body and bride), there is one faith, one hope, and one baptism (Eph. 4:5). Luther reconceptualizes this faith by bending it back to the believer—what theologian Paul Hacker calls *reflexive faith.*

According to [Luther], what properly justifies is not simply faith in God or Christ. Only the reflection, qualified by certitude, that God's salvific deed is meant "for me" works salvation, and this reflection brings about its effect infallibly. . . . The complete "realization" of this "*pro me,*" this "for me" . . . comes about by way of a "bending back" of the consciousness to the believing self. Without this reflexivity, justifying faith would be indistinguishable from what Luther dismisses as a testimonial belief in the facticity of certain events (*fides historica*).[113]

Luther's reflexive faith changes the emphasis of faith from believing in Christ to believing in what Christ has done *for me personally, as an individual.*

This change from faith to *reflexive* faith has far-reaching implications and laid the groundwork for the atheist and materialist philosopher Ludwig Feuerbach (1804–1872), who claims that God is nothing more than a projection of our own wants and needs. Religion, therefore, is "exclusively anthropocentric." Still later, this idea will morph into *moralistic therapeutic deism.*[114]

Apostolicity Reimagined

The notion of apostolicity also undergoes a radical change under Luther. Apostolicity is changed from being a visible, continuous succession of bishops who attest to and hand on what they were given by the inspired apostles to a collection of individuals identified only by preaching Christ

156

and his gospel—as Luther understands it. As Luther writes:

> So our papists boast of their number, their traditional right, the continuity of centuries, the apostolic sees. We must answer them: "God is truthful. Those who believe in Him are the church and the godly, even though they are the least and the fewest."[115]

Luther effectively severs Christ as head from his body. We learn of Christ no longer through his body, which is a visible, historical, identifiable, structured community of disciples, but through Luther's gospel. If someone preaches the truth—as Luther understands it—then that person is authentically apostolic. If he doesn't preach as Luther preaches, he is not apostolic, regardless of if he can trace his teaching back to the apostles.[116]

Luther and Scripture

Luther's redefinition of apostolicity ultimately undermines Scripture. How do we know which books are inspired? Augustine answered that we know through the visible apostolic Church:

> Now, in regard to the canonical scriptures, we must follow the judgment of the greater number of Catholic churches; and among these, of course, *a high place must be given to such as have been thought worthy to be the seat of an apostle and to receive epistles.*[117]

The correct canon of Scripture is anchored in the historic Church. Luther, however, unmoors Scripture from its historical foundation and places it on subjective ground. He writes:

> Now it is the office of a true apostle to preach of the Passion and resurrection and office of Christ, and to lay the foundation for faith in him. . . . *All the genuine sacred books agree in this, that all of them preach and inculcate [treiben] Christ.* And that is *the true test* by which to judge *all books*, when we see whether or not they inculcate Christ. . . . *Whatever does not teach Christ is not yet apostolic, even though St. Peter or St. Paul does the teaching.* Again, whatever preaches Christ would be apostolic, *even if Judas, Annas, Pilate, and Herod were doing it.*[118]

This is in stark contrast to Peter's words:

> For we did not follow cleverly devised myths when we made known to you the power and coming of our Lord Jesus Christ, but we were eyewitnesses. . . . *We* were with him on the holy mountain. And *we* have the prophetic word made more sure (2 Pet. 1:16,18–19, emphasis mine).

So the gospel—*as Luther understands it*—is proposed as the norm for determining what is and what is not genuine Scripture.

De-Sacralizing the Church

Luther's focus on an unmediated relationship with God by knowing his will through Scripture alone effectively displaces things like sacramentals, the priesthood, and even the sacraments.[119] The sacraments are not seven—as defined at the Council of Florence in 1439—but three: baptism, the Eucharist, and a modified version of confession (see Pope Eugenius IV, *Exsultate Domine* [Decree for the Armenians], Council of Florence, 1439). These three sacraments are defined as visible signs to which the promise of grace is attached. This is quite different from the Catholic understanding of the sacraments producing what they signify.

One of the first things Luther changes is the Mass—and with it, the priesthood. He retains a belief in the real substantial presence of Christ in the Eucharist, but he denies that the Mass is a sacrifice offered by a priest.

In fact, the words of consecration—"this is my body" and "this cup is my blood"—are not as important as the words "which is given for you" and "which is shed for you for the forgiveness of sin." Luther's *Small Catechism* asks, "How can bodily eating and drinking do such a great thing?" The answer:

Eating and drinking certainly do not in themselves produce them, but the words "for you," and "for the forgiveness of sin." These words, when accompanied by the bodily eating and drinking, are the chief thing in the sacrament, and he who believes these words has what they say and declare: the forgiveness of sin.[120]

It isn't the consuming of the incarnate Christ (body, blood, soul, and divinity) that brings about "the forgiveness of sin, life, and salvation," but one's *reflexive faith* in the words "given *for you*" and "shed *for you*." These words, plus the consuming of the Eucharist, make the benefits come about.

Luther also reduces holy orders to the common priesthood given at baptism:

> As far as that goes, we are all consecrated priests through baptism. . . . Therefore, when a bishop consecrates it is nothing else than that in the place and stead of the whole community, all of whom have like power, he takes a person and charges him to exercise this power on behalf of the others.[121]

Priests reduced to simple ministers in this way become not at all different from a baptized cobbler, prince, or farmer. The only difference is that they are charged "to exercise this power on behalf of others." Luther hopes this institutionalized Christian egalitarianism will spell the demise of the papacy.[122] Instead, as we will see later, it spells the disintegration of Protestantism.

Sacramentals

Luther's rejection of relics, indulgences, prayers for the dead, etc. severs the Church Triumphant and the Church Suffering from the Church Militant on earth. It also severs Christians from each other. No longer is Christianity a society where members of the body can mystically bear each other's suffering and share spiritual benefits. It becomes a collection of individuals united only in a common belief that Christ died for them.

Love and Unity Lost

Luther's teaching of justification by faith alone separates faith from the other theological virtues of hope and love, which causes a problem when it comes to assurance: if we are justified by faith alone apart from love and good works, how do we know we are truly justified? What anchors our confidence that we have saving faith? Are we justified because *we believe* we are justified?[123]

Earlier, we saw how Christ associates himself with his body so as to make love a salvation issue. At the Final Judgment (Matt. 25), Jesus teaches, we will be judged according to our works (whether we clothe the naked, feed the hungry, visit the imprisoned, care for the sick, etc.), not by whether we had reflexive faith. Luther's views on justification, therefore, change the emphasis from self-giving to knowledge of one's personal salvation. The result is a loss of charity and love among his followers, a fact even Luther recognizes.[124]

Loss of Unity

The most obvious and devastating effect of Luther's revolt is the loss of unity. At the outset of the Reformation, disagreements begin between Luther and the Swiss Protestant reformer Ulrich Zwingli (1484–1531) over the Eucharist.

At a meeting known as the Marburg Colloquy (October 1–4, 1529), both parties attempt to reconcile. One portion of this dialogue from the Colloquy is instructive:

> "Again and again the body of Christ is eaten, for he himself commands us so," Luther replied. "If he ordered me to eat manure, I would do it, since I would altogether know that it would be my salvation. Let not the bond servant brood over the will of the Master. We have to close our eyes." . . . When he was asked if he recognized the others as his brothers, Luther shouted: "Your spirit and our spirit do not go together. . . . For there cannot be the same spirit if one side simply believes the words of Christ and the other side reprimands, attacks, denies and blasphemes this faith."[125]

Luther's words echo Ockham's assertion that God could have crucified an ass, and it would have sufficed for the salvation of the world, although the contexts are different. Luther and Zwingli appeal to the same text but interpret it according to different spirits. Which spirit is the Holy Spirit? They can't both be right. Christ either is or is not substantially present in the Eucharist. In the end, the Marburg Colloquy shows that the two sides are irreconcilable on this point.

Righteous Rebel

Protestant disunity isn't an accident; it is woven into the DNA of Luther's break from the Church. It cannot fail to produce schisms and disunity because Luther's fundamental reasons for breaking from the Church—doctrinal purity and the freedom of conscience (whether it be unformed, ill formed, or self-formed)—are divisive.

Luther uttered his most renowned saying at the imperial assembly at the Diet of Worms (1521):

Unless I am convinced by the testimony of the Scriptures or by clear reason (for I do not trust either in the pope or in councils alone, since it is well known that they have often erred and contradicted themselves), I am bound by the Scriptures I have quoted and *my conscience is captive to the Word of God.* I cannot and I will not retract anything, since it is neither safe nor right to go against conscience. I cannot do otherwise, here I stand, may God help me, amen.[126]

Although we should never violate our conscience, we have a duty to form our conscience in accord with what is true. Luther's conscience was formed by what he believed Scripture taught or by what he believed was right reason. But if Luther, for conscience's sake, can rebel against the historic Church because he believes that it has erred, what will prevent others, for conscience's sake, from rebelling against Luther because it appears to them that Luther has erred? Luther cannot claim the right of conscience for himself and deny it to others. Protestantism does not rid itself of an infallible pope; rather, it makes every Protestant an infallible pope unto himself.

Luther's reaction to the rapid disintegration of Protestant unity is instructive:

> This won't have baptism, that denies the efficacy of the Lord's Supper; a third, puts a world between this and the Last Judgment; others teach that Jesus Christ is not God; some say this, others that; and *there are almost as many sects and beliefs as there are heads. . . . When the pope reigned we heard nothing of these troubles.*[127]

Luther's words—"there are almost as many sects and beliefs as there are heads"—sound remarkably similar to St. Vincent of Lérins's comments regarding heretical interpretations of Scripture: "that it seems to be capable of as many interpretations as there are interpreters."[128] Vincent continues: "For Novatian expounds it one way, Sabellius another, Donatus another, Arius, Eunomius, Macedonius, another." One could replace these old heretical sects with those of Luther's day: "For Lutherans expound it one way, Zwinglians another, Anabaptists another, Calvinists another."

Even after Protestantism rejects Luther and his teachings, the figure of him standing against the historic Church at Worms will become emblematic of what it means to be Protestant: standing alone, fighting for your own beliefs. This *holy rebel* paradigm will become part of the Protestant identity. And each Protestant sect will experience multiple Diet of Worms moments, when its individual members take their stand and break away, forming their own denominations, congregations, and sects.

GOVERNMENT
Two Kingdoms

In addition to Luther's dichotomies—the body and soul, law and gospel, works and faith, the outward man and the inward man—he adds yet another by cleaving the government into the spiritual and the temporal. This dichotomy is known as Luther's doctrine of *two kingdoms*.

> God has ordained the two governments: the spiritual, which by the Holy Spirit under Christ makes Christians and pious people; and the secular, which restrains the unchristian and wicked so that they are obliged to keep the peace outwardly. . . . The laws of worldly government extend no farther than to life and property and what is external upon earth. For over the soul God can and will let no one rule but himself. Therefore, where temporal power presumes to prescribe laws for the soul, it encroaches upon God's government and only misleads and destroys souls.[129]

The *two kingdoms* idea fits perfectly within Luther's bifurcated world. Luther's compartmentalizing of worldly affairs from the interior affairs of faith opens the door to a similar move by John Locke, where religion becomes a distinct, separate, and ultimately subordinate sphere of human life.

HUMAN KNOWLEDGE
No-Popery History Begins

Luther's claim that he has rediscovered the gospel raises an obvious question: how could the historic Church have been so misled over all the centuries regarding such crucial data? Luther is aware of this problem and takes measures to solve it, such as redefining apostolicity in a non-historical sense. Still, the historic Church remains the elephant in the room.

True, the Church certainly isn't perfect, but it *is* the Church. Luther's new worldview needs more than fiery religious rhetoric to exhort Catholics to turn against the Church of their youth. It needs substance to back it up. History needs to be retold.

Matthias Vlacich (known as Flacius) (1520–1575) is the man for the job. As a young man, Flacius has a religious calling and even considers entering the monastic life. However, his uncle, an apostate friar, has different ideas. He poisons young Flacius's views on Catholicism and encourages him to travel to Germany and join the Protestant uprising. Flacius does just that. He excels in learning and becomes known as a staunch, somewhat rigid Lutheran with an extreme anti-Catholic bent.

After Luther's death, Flacius focuses his attention on attacking the Catholic Church through history. He writes his *Catalogue of Witnesses of the Truth*, which sports four hundred witnesses against the papal Antichrist.[130] This book lays the groundwork for a more comprehensive anti-Catholic history, with a much longer title.[131] For purposes of space, we will call it just *Centuries*. Flacius's *Centuries* divides history into hundred-year periods, and each member of the writing team is assigned one century to cover; hence, its authors are known as the *Magdeburg Centuriators*.

To its credit, Flacius's *Centuries* often uses primary sources. However, the overall focus of the work is incredibly biased and cut to fit Luther's vision of history, where the Church has gone astray by being misled by the Antichrist—in this case, the pope.

> Consequently as early as the second century errors are discovered in the teachings of Clement, Justin Martyr and Irenaeus on the fundamental doctrines of free will and justification.[132]

Although the project deserves a measure of praise for its use of original sources and the amount of material it marshaled, the *Centuries*' polemical aims nevertheless cripple its value as a historical resource.

> Its constant polemical tone, its grouping of facts colored by party spirit, its unjust treatment of the Church, its uncritical accumulation of anti-papal story and legend, made the "Centuries" for a long time the arsenal, of Protestant controversialists.[133]

Flacius's *Centuries* integrates solid historical data with myths, legends, and scandalous rumors. Some of these myths, such as the Pope Joan myth, survive today despite centuries of debunking.[134]

Catholics feel a need to answer the Centuriators on solid historical grounds. The lot falls to Caesar Baronius (1538–1607), who spends most of his life responding to the Centuriators' calumnies.

Baronius is a man of immense learning. His project is the *Annales Ecclesiastici a Christo nato ad annum* (1198).[135] His attention to detail delays the project considerably, and the publication of the first comprehensive response to Flacius's *Centuries* doesn't appear until almost two decades later. By then, the Lutheran *Centuries* has become the foundation for the ever-growing edifice of no-popery history.

Ulrich Zwingli

One of the first to part ways with Luther is the Protestant Swiss reformer Ulrich Zwingli (1484–1531). Zwingli is a Catholic priest who, like Luther, revolts against the Church. In 1519, the same year Luther admits that councils can and do err and that the Deuterocanon is not canonical Scripture, Zwingli adopts the idea of the Bible as Christianity's sole authority (*sola scriptura*).

Zwingli's main focus is to divest the Faith of its sacramentality and materiality. His work touches on all seven areas we have been focusing on in this book. His homilies target corruption within the hierarchy, the veneration of the saints, hellfire, the denial that tithing is divinely instituted, and the power of excommunication.

After petitioning the bishop to abolish clerical celibacy (he had been secretly married the year before), Zwingli continues his preaching against the use of images and the Mass, even persuading the city council in Zurich to enforce his exhortations by law. He also spearheads the suppression of the monasteries, which serve the poor, replacing their charitable work with a welfare system.

Just as Luther experienced in Germany, some of Zwingli's followers believe that he hasn't gone far enough and seek doctrinal clarity. They advocate that the civil authority be replaced by a council of believers. Under the leadership of Conrad Grebel (1498–1526), a new *Anabaptist* movement begins in Zurich, which calls for the prohibition of infant baptism and the institution of believer's (adult) baptism only.

Zwingli and the city council won't hear of it, and on August 15, 1524, the city council passes an ordinance requiring all infants to be baptized. The Anabaptists ignore the law, performing the first adult re-baptism on January 21, 1525. In response, the council enacts a law that anyone who re-baptizes another will be put to death. A few Anabaptists are executed by drowning; the rest flee the city.

Christ's Humanity Disappears Yet Again

Earlier, we examined the Marburg Colloquy (October 1–4, 1529), where Zwingli and Luther attempted to reconcile but could not agree on the Eucharist. Luther believed in the real substantial presence of Christ in the Eucharist, whereas Zwingli believed that the Eucharist is a mere memorial or symbol.

Christology was at the heart of this dispute. Each side accused the other of denying or distorting Christ's humanity. Luther claimed that Christ's humanity participates in the divine attribute of omnipresence, so his body can be everywhere God wills it to be. The problem here, as Ludwig

Ott explains, is that

> the old Lutheran doctrinal theology inclines to the Mono-
> physitic error which posits a real transference of divine
> attributes such as omniscience, omnipotence, ubiquity,
> by reason of the hypostatic union, to the human nature
> of Christ, and teaches that "Christ, not only as God, but
> also *as man* knows all, can do all, and is present to all cre-
> ated things."[136]

The problem of Monophysitism is that by combining
Christ's divine and human natures, his humanity is no longer human. It becomes a third nature that is neither fully
divine nor fully human. Zwingli therefore rejected it.

Luther, on the other hand, accused Zwingli of deni-
grating Christ's humanity by refusing to recognize it in
the Eucharist. Indeed, Zwingli's view promoted a kind of
Gnosticism where partaking of Christ's body and blood is
reduced to knowledge:

> "*Credere est edere*," said Zwingli: "To believe is to eat."
> To eat the body and to drink the blood of Christ in the
> Supper, then, simply meant to have the body and blood
> of Christ present in the mind.[137]

Zwingli's denial of the Real Presence split reality in two.
As Alister McGrath wrote:

Where Catholicism allowed a direct encounter between the believer and spiritual realities, Zwingli resolutely refused to acknowledge that spiritual realities could ever be known through the material world. Christ was in heaven; Christian worship was about recalling what Christ had done in the past and looking forward to his future return. But in the present—in the here and now—Christ was known only as an absence.[138]

McGrath's words are on point. Zwingli sought not only to rid the Eucharist of Christ's substantial presence. He also wished to strip Christ's body, the Church, of its sacramentality by exchanging visible religion for an invisible religion—one without a hierarchy, images, the Mass, the veneration of saints, or the distinctiveness of a celibate clergy.

The Radical Reformation

The Anabaptists aren't only in Zurich; they spring up throughout Europe. The name *Anabaptist* comes from a Greek word that means "baptize again." Their distinct character is a radical reductionist approach to Christian belief and practice. Anything not found on the pages of Scripture is to be rejected or held in suspicion, with the most odious of all being infant baptism. Since infant baptism is not explicitly mentioned in the New Testament and salvation is to come by faith alone, the Anabaptists believe that only those capable of faith (i.e., older children and adults) can be baptized.

Like Zwingli, the Anabaptists deny Christ's substantial

presence in the Eucharist, and they promote the destruction of religious images. But as we saw above, they go beyond Zwingli in their reductionism, raising even Zwingli's ire. Believing themselves, like Luther, to be guided by God as the sole arbiters of truth to re-establish pure Christianity, they attempt to transform the world. One instance of this otherworldly transformation will take the revolt against reality to another level of insanity—namely, through the Münster prophets.

The Münster Prophets

The city of Münster in Germany is under Lutheran control, and like all Lutheran territories, it is anti-Catholic. A small group there, headed by the Lutheran pastor Bernhard Rothmann (1495–1535), fiercely attacks Catholicism through a popular pamphlet campaign. Over time, the pamphlets' contents become more and more radical, eventually announcing that the Bible calls for the absolute equality of all men in every respect, including wealth. As these pamphlets circulate in northern Germany, and after the Peasants' War (1524–1525), teams of poor people flood into the region to share the wealth and become part of the new kingdom of God.

With the influx of supporters, Rothmann and his group have no problems winning elections and installing Bernhard Knipperdolling (1495–1536) as mayor. Their first move is to depose all the Lutheran magistrates who had once supported the group's anti-Catholicism, since these people are now seen as obstacles to furthering their agenda. Hearing that

Rothmann is teaching similar doctrines, more Anabaptists come into the city and eventually begin mass "rebaptisms." As Lutherans flee, the inhabitants unleash a campaign of iconoclasm against cathedrals and monasteries. Eventually, adult baptisms are made compulsory, and all property is mandated to be shared in common.

In response, the expelled prince-bishop Franz von Waldeck (1491-1553), who is more Lutheran than Catholic, and more a prince than a bishop, along with the Catholics who were expelled from the city, lays siege to Münster. Within the city walls, things become more unhinged.

Jan Matthys (1500–1534), one of the Münster leaders, claims that he received a prophecy that God is going to smite the evil men besieging the city, so he runs out with twelve of his followers to miraculously slay the infidel. The thirteen are immediately slaughtered. Matthys's head is cut off and placed on a pole before the city, and his genitals are nailed to the city gates.

John of Leiden (1509–1536) is elected Matthys's successor and the self-proclaimed king of the New Jerusalem. During his reign, he permits Münster's inhabitants to take multiple wives. John himself has sixteen.

On June 24, 1535, Münster is taken. The leaders are tortured and executed, and their bodies are kept in cages hung on the steeple of the local church.

John Calvin

Luther was anything but systematic and coherent in his theology. His thoughts were a labyrinth of inconsistent and even contradictory teachings. Indeed, Protestantism may not have survived if it weren't for John Calvin (1509–1564), whose genius is to take his Protestant insights and put them into a single coherent theological system. The result: *The Institutes of the Christian Religion.*

God's "Hidden Justice"

Is Calvin a nominalist? Early Protestant research suggests that he was, but recent studies have called this into question, at least in part. There is no doubt that Calvin is influenced by nominalist teaching. Does his teaching reflect nominalism? Sometimes yes and sometimes no. There are portions of his writings that seem to reject nominalism, or at least speak favorably of some scholastic teaching. But there are other parts where his nominalism is unmistakable.

Imputed Righteousness

Calvin follows Luther in holding that justification is by faith alone. As Reformed theologian Hans Boersma writes:

> Calvin, much like Luther, was intent on keeping justification separate from human works. In order to do this, he, too, maintained that justification was a nominal or external judicial declaration rather than an internal transformation worked by the Holy Spirit. The underlying pattern of the Reformation doctrine, with its strong focus

on imputation, would not have been possible without the nominalist developments of the late Middle Ages.[139]

God's sovereign decree, not one's union with Christ's body or participation in his grace, is the essence of becoming right with God. Grace is conceived mainly as God's favorable disposition toward someone and only secondarily as participation in his life and power in sanctification.

Whereas Luther's focus was mainly against Catholicism and the separation of faith from works, Calvin's focus is to protect the transcendence and sovereignty of God over creation. If grace is mainly God's favor, and justification is a legal decree by which righteousness is imputed to us, whatever is left—the outward physical trappings, devotions, and other human things—can get in the way of God's sovereignty.

Double Power/Double Justice

A key aspect of nominalism is to separate God's will from his nature and make a distinction between God's ordinary or ordained will (how he usually wills) and his absolute will (the ability to will anything he desires). Calvin is critical of this distinction. In fact, he rejects some applications of it as blasphemy. He also rejects the idea that God's will is somehow separated from his attributes, especially justice.[140] Instead, Calvin substitutes a distinction that essentially does the same thing. He proposes that there is a double justice that distinguishes God's will, as it is revealed to man, from God's *hidden justice*, which is a higher and unknowable justice above the Law:

> Calvin gradually becomes uneasy with his own theory
> of twofold justice. Although this hermeneutical device
> allows him to explain various passages, it also leaves him
> with a terrifying question: Can God override the lower
> justice and judge according to the rigor of his secret
> justice? Having made use of the now developed theory
> of the twofold justice, Calvin is caught. Although Cal-
> vin's [interpretation of the book of] Job gained a deeper
> understanding of God's justice, he was forced to the brink
> where he glimpsed a God who, acting "without cause,"
> might be "playing with men like balls." Calvin's increas-
> ing discomfort is more evident in his awareness that the
> distinction between revealed and secret justice looks
> suspiciously like that dreaded "nominalist" distinction
> between absolute and ordained power.[141]

Calvin's double justice idea is also useful in that it makes
his teaching that God eternally predestines some to heaven
and some to hell more palatable. If God predestines some to
hell, then they will necessarily live a life worthy of damna-
tion. But how can God be good and just for punishing the
reprobate for sins he could not avoid?

Boersma explains:

> Calvin is aware of the objection that reprobation "is more
> like the caprice of a tyrant than the lawful sentence of a

judge." In his defense, Calvin makes the will of God the ultimate court of appeal: "For God's will is so much the highest rule of righteousness that whatever he wills, by the very fact that he wills it, must be considered righteous." God appears to will things not because they are just, but they are just because God will them. It is difficult to escape the idea that God stands outside the law (*ex lex*).[142]

Calvin insists that God's will is not arbitrary. It is rooted in his nature and attributes. However, he also proposes in double justice that God's attributes, such as justice, are on a different order completely unknown and unknowable to us. But this makes God's hidden justice indistinguishable from an arbitrary will, at least from our perspective.

Assurance of Predestination to Glory

When Theodore Beza (1519–1605) reformulates Calvin's theology, he centers it on God's double predestination (either to heaven or to hell) and raises an important question: how does one know whether one has been predestined to glory or not? This was especially difficult to answer for Calvin, since he raised the possibility that one may have an "ineffectual calling" or a temporary faith. As Calvin wrote:

There are two species of calling: for there is a universal call, by which God, through the external preaching of the word, invites all men alike, even those for whom he designs the call to be a savor of death, and the ground of a severer condemnation. Besides this there is a special call which, for the most part, God bestows on believers only, when by the internal illumination of the Spirit he causes the word preached to take deep root in their hearts. Sometimes, however, he communicates it also to those whom *he enlightens only for a time*, and whom afterwards, in just punishment for their ingratitude, *he abandons and smites with greater blindness.*[143]

From our perspective, it's impossible to know whether the enlightenment one receives from the gospel is permanent and effectual or temporary and ultimately ineffectual, since both give all the outward signs of being genuine. Appearances, therefore, do not necessarily correspond to a spiritual reality. Indeed, the enlightenment of the Holy Spirit may deceive people into thinking they are destined for heaven.

One Power in Salvation and Christ

Christ's true humanity also becomes a problem within Calvinism. A key idea within Calvinist thought is called *monergism*, the belief that only God works or operates in salvation. This is opposed to *synergism*, which holds that human cooperation has a part.

Calvinists hold a variety of opinions as to how widely monergism should be understood and applied, but the gist of it is this: Since God is not, in any way, dependent upon his creation or creatures, according to Calvin, any human co-operation is nothing more than what God predestined and brought about. It is not free.

Although monergism attempts to guarantee God's absolute sovereignty over creation, it actually conceives of creation as being in competition with its Creator. God's freedom and human freedom are pitted against each other, like two people eating slices from the same apple pie. The more slices one person eats, the fewer slices are left for the other. Therefore, if there is anything other than God operating in the cosmos (like human free will), then God is not truly free, nor is he truly God. A non-monergistic cosmos is impossible under the Calvinist understanding.

Calvinist monergism has drastic consequences when it is applied to the Incarnation. How should we understand Christ's human will? Was it truly free, or was it predestined by the Father? Author Robin Philips comments:

> If we say that Christ's human will was exempt from divine predestination, then it is hard to avoid the implication that there must have been true non-monergistic synergy and co-operation between the divine and the human wills of Christ. But if so, then it is equally hard to see why it would be problematic to assert a similar non-monergistic synergy and co-operation between the divine and the human wills when dealing with the rest of humanity, especially since Christ typified the appropriate relation between humanity and divinity.[144]

If Christ's human will was nothing more than a passive instrument irresistibly moved by his divine will, we find ourselves back in the radical Monothelite camp mentioned earlier, which implies that Christ's saving work on the cross was not meritorious. Since merit is possible only by something capable of moving toward perfection, only an authentic free human will can do something truly meritorious.[145]

Calvin's solution is to argue that Christ's death and obedience were meritorious—not in themselves, but by divine decree:

> The free favor of God is as fitly opposed to our works *as is the obedience of Christ*, both in their order: *for Christ could not merit anything save by the good pleasure of God*, but only inasmuch as *he was destined* to appease the wrath of God by his sacrifice, and wipe away our transgressions *by his obedience*: in one word, since the merit of Christ depends entirely on the grace of God (which provided this mode of salvation for us), the latter is no less appropriately opposed to all righteousness of men than is the former.[146]

Here we see the nominalist idea that God declares nonmeritorious actions meritorious in his sight, even though, in truth, they are not. One also wonders how Calvin can speak about Christ's obedience, since his human will is destined to obey God. It would be like calling a chair obedient because it does what it is destined to do by its construction. The word is robbed of its meaning.

Philips concludes:

> To be consistent Calvinism must deny that the human will possesses such self-determining powers. Thus, Christ's obedience to the Father to the point of death becomes either a kind of fake dramatization or something attributed to his divine nature only. The notion that the humanity of Christ was simply a passive tool surfaces now and again in contemporary Reformed polemics.[147]

The desire to prevent creation or human agency from impinging on God's sovereignty also impacts Calvin's idea of Christian life and worship.

THE CHURCH

De-Sacralizing Time and Space

Calvin's renovation of his home church, Saint-Pierre, in 1543 reflects his view that material things are an impediment to contact with the divine. Calvin has the walls whitewashed, covers pictures and icons, and places the pulpit at the center:

> The simplicity of the churches was designed to concentrate the eye and mind of worshippers on the service. The whitewashed walls rejected any material mediation of the

divine and emphasized its immanence.[148]

Calvin's renovation can't strip all material mediation from Saint-Pierre. There is still the mediation of the minister—his voice, his body motions, his interpretation and presentation of Scripture, the congregations' ears and eyes. Even these will be replaced in future revolts by the interior disposition of the soul.

Calvin also locks the church building when there isn't a service so people will not come in to pray. Such a thing strikes Calvin as superstitious, since it suggests that some places are intrinsically more sacred than others. Christian life is to be stripped of sacred space.[149] Theologian William Dyrness notes:

> The pulpit and the table were all that remained in St. Peter's church, and the table was set only during Communion. What, then, of the place in which this took place? It was the stage on which the performance of worship was played out, and when that was finished, the place had no further role to play. . . . Worship was everywhere, but it was nowhere in particular.[150]

Not only is sacred space suppressed, but so is sacred time. Calvin sees the observances of holy days, except for Sunday, also as superstition. In his Christmas Day sermon in 1551, he preaches:

Now, I see here today more people that I am accustomed to having at the sermon. Why is that? It is Christmas Day. And who told you this? You poor beasts. That is a fitting euphemism for all of you who have come here today to honor Noel. . . . For when you elevate one day alone for the purpose of worshipping God, you have just turned it into an idol. True, you insist that you have done so for the honor of God, but it is more for the honor of the devil.[151]

The sanctification of time goes back to the Old Testament. God set special times for fasting, penance, and celebration. Christianity, the fulfillment of Judaism, naturally recognized sacred time and modeled its liturgical calendar after the life of Christ. It was through this practice that time itself came into subjection to Christ.

Calvin's rejection of the calendar does just the opposite. As McGrath notes:

For Protestants, especially those tracing their lineage back to Calvin and Zwingli, there can no sense of sacred space or place—no possibility of a direct encounter with the sacred or an experience of the divine other than that which is mediated indirectly through reading the Bible and the public exposition of its message.[152]

Not everyone is on board with Calvin's desacralization of time. The city magistrates insist on keeping holy days, since they regulate days off for workers.[153]

The suppression of the liturgical calendar creates a vacuum that secularism is glad to fill. Today, holy days have become holidays. The vacuum left by Reformed Protestantism has been filled by consumerism, Easter bunnies, Santa Claus, and "Hallmark holidays." In the words of Clark W. Griswold of *Christmas Vacation* fame: Christmas "means something different to everybody."

The English Reformation

Unlike the Continental Reformation, which is led by a few religious revolutionaries who, through the protection of local princes, gain control over territories, England's reformation comes from the top down.

King Henry VIII (1491–1547) is a Catholic sovereign who vigorously seeks to protect his realm from Lutheran and other Protestant influence. Indeed, he even publishes a work on *The Defense of the Seven Sacraments* (1521) for which the pope awards him the title *Defensor Fidei* (Defender of the Faith) in October of the same year. England's break with the Church centers not so much on doctrine as on discipline.

MARRIAGE AND FAMILY
Divorce Returns

Henry is married to Catherine of Aragon, his brother's widow. The couple are unable to produce a male heir. Mindful of the past civil wars caused by rival claims to the throne, Henry petitions the pope to grant a decree of nullity so he can marry another woman. Pope Clement VII refuses. As a result, Henry breaks from the Church and, through the *Act of Supremacy* (1534), makes himself the "supreme head on earth of the Church of England." Henry now wields both the temporal and the spiritual sword in his land.

Since the English Reformation is complex, we are forced to set down a few key points that advance the revolt against reason and eventually reality itself.

THE CHURCH

The Branch Theory

The belief that the Church is a historic, visible, tangible, identifiable society rooted in the apostles continues after the *Act of Supremacy*. The problem is reconciling Henry's break from Rome with that notion. One theory that attempts to solve this problem is known as the *branch theory*, which reconceptualizes the Church of England as being one branch, along with the Orthodox and Roman branches. Each branch is said to be equally self-ruling, yet they are all part of the same tree.

The branch theory not only denies the universal jurisdiction of the pope, but also does away with the unity of the body. Not only, under this theory, is each branch autonomous (which has no parallel to the members of a healthy body), but England's fusion of Church and State will force it to tolerate theological disunity and eventually put it farther outside of the teachings of the historic Church.

State and Church Fusion

The moral authority of the Church, however modest and infrequent its successes, functions to cap the authority of the State. Sovereigns are not free to do whatever they wish. They, being Christians, are just as obligated to follow the gospel as their citizens. For this reason, the State always tries to gain some measure of control over the Church. The investiture controversies are a good example of these tensions. When Henry makes himself head of both Church and State in England, he effectively removes all capping authority. He can do whatever he can get Parliament (and anyone else who fears for his life) to go along with.

The fusion of Church and State is devastating for both. In a normal State-Church government, the separation of powers supports the established religion while tolerating religious minorities to various degrees. Sects, like the Albigensians, are suppressed when they become a threat to the State; otherwise, they are generally tolerated. In England, however, no real toleration can be meted out, since to oppose the Church is the same as opposing the State. True patriots are expected to be members of the established church; seditious rebels operate outside it.

Since not every person who holds differing views about religion is necessarily seditious, the Church of England needs to be doctrinally broad enough to accommodate dissenting religious claims. This turns the English church into a crucible of competing and contrary religious groups battling for dominance or just survival within its structure. The end result is to produce an incoherent mishmash of doctrines and practices under the umbrella of a church. Some factions worship with a Latin liturgy; others prefer no liturgy. Some believe in the Real Presence of Christ in the Eucharist; others believe that it is merely symbolic. These and everything in between are countenanced as long as there is no threat to the Church-State (i.e., nothing Catholic). The long-term effects of radically different religious perspectives being countenanced under the umbrella of *Church* can't help but contribute to the belief that there is no objective Christian norm for faith and practice, that doctrine is nothing more than a political football. The roller coaster ride of changing sovereigns and religious stances further underscores these views.

Changing Monarchs and Religions

When Henry VIII founds the Church of England, he leaves Catholic doctrines largely intact. His successor, Edward VI (1537–1553), is nine years old when he takes the throne, and he is the first monarch to be raised Protestant. Under him, clerical celibacy is abolished, and attendance at Protestant services is made compulsory.

Edward dies at the age of fifteen. His successor, Mary I (1516–1558), is the only child of Henry VIII and Catherine of Aragon. She is Catholic and reverses the Edwardian changes, bringing England back into communion with Rome. Then Elizabeth I (1558–1603), who follows Mary, reverses her reforms, re-establishing the Church of England and making herself the head.

Along with changing sovereigns comes a changing liturgy. When Parliament passes the *Uniformity Act* (1559), replacing the Latin Mass with the English *Book of Common Prayer* (passing by only three votes), it is "the third time in 12 years, pastors, parishes, and congregants had to change the forms and order of worship."[154]

The constant back and forth, revisions, and changes can only dampen religious fervor by making the Faith look like a plaything for rulers rather than the extension of the Incarnation through the centuries.

Monasteries Suppressed

Once Henry VIII becomes the spiritual head of the country, the duty of inspecting the monasteries, which hold large portions of land in England, is taken from the charge of the bishops and given to the crown.

Thomas Cromwell [is] the king's vicar-general in spirituals, with special authority to visit the monastic houses, and to bring them into line with the new order of things. This was in 1534; and, some time prior to the December of that year, arrangements were already being made for a systematic visitation. . . . The monasteries were doomed prior to these visitations, and not in consequence of them, as we have been asked to believe according to the traditional story. Parliament was to meet early in the following year, 1536, and, with the twofold object of replenishing an exhausted exchequer and of anticipating opposition on the part of the religious to the proposed ecclesiastical changes, according to the royal design, the Commons were to be asked to grant Henry the possessions of at least the smaller monasteries. . . . A project such as this must be sustained by strong yet simple reasons calculated to appeal to the popular mind. Some decent pretext had to be found for presenting the proposed measure of suppression and confiscation to the nation, and it can hardly now be doubted that the device of blackening the characters of the monks and nuns was deliberately resorted to.[155]

Suppressed religious houses are not just vacated, but ransacked to squeeze out every last penny. Everything is stripped and sold, down to frames, shutters, doors, gutters, and rain pipes.[156] Within a few years, the suppression extends to the larger monasteries as well.

The suppression of the monasteries is not an attempt to reform religious life, but a thinly veiled cash grab. The money received through the suppression goes in part to the monks' retirement and then into the crown's purse. These lands and other goods are in turn used to secure the loyalty of the nobles.

Charity to Welfare

The suppression of monasteries is not unique in England.

Lutheran and Calvinist lands do the same thing. However, the suppression in England is different; it is not driven by anti-Catholic popular support. The English generally do not hold ill feelings against the monasteries, nor is there a groundswell of support for their suppression. In fact, in the summer of 1535, the crown commissions *railers* and preachers to go throughout the country to change public opinion against the monasteries.[157] The public strongly resist and resent the suppression, especially in Northern England, where there are large-scale protests under the title *Pilgrimage of Grace*. The motivation for the suppression comes from the top down: from the king and his supporters.

As we have seen, the monasteries are places for religious to live in community to work and pray. They serve an important role in extending Christian charity to the poor. Wealthy benefactors donate money and goods to the monasteries for the temporal care of the poor, and the poor, in turn, provide prayers for the souls of their benefactors in thanksgiving for their charity. The monastery, along with local parishes, is at the center of this economy of love. The suppression of the monasteries destroys this beautiful economy, leaving the poor to fend for themselves and the burden of their care to the local parishes, which don't enjoy the monasteries' economy of scale.

Although the suppression leaves Catholic hospitals intact, it cuts off their means of income, creating a financial crisis for large hospitals operating in the city of London. Henry VIII is forced to endow the hospitals on the condition that the city pays for their operating expenses. When the city is unable to do so, it institutes a compulsory tax, called the Poor Rate, in 1547, which replaces Sunday collections with a mandatory collection for the poor.[158] Later, another piece of legislation, *The Acte for the Reliefe of the Poore* (1597–98), compels each parish to have its churchwarden and four overseers employ sturdy beggars (the able-bodied poor), provide relief for the elderly and infirm, start apprenticeships for poor children seven years old and older, and tax the people within the parish to pay for these services.[159]

The suppression of the monasteries transforms the voluntary charitable support for the poor and the sick into a government program, complete with a compulsory tax at the parish level. Compulsory charity may sound familiar. We saw how Julian the Apostate attempted to reform paganism by mandating that pagan priests feed the poor through government subsidies. This is not to suggest that England has become pagan or that the English aren't charitable. Rather, it shows that England has turned a corner. Christian charity has been replaced by a government mandate. These early Poor Laws lay the groundwork for the modern welfare state.

From Poor Tax to Welfare to Population Control

Although we are jumping ahead to a later chapter in our rebellion, it's important that we follow this thread a little farther. Unlike the pagans, who viewed the poor as those fated to be lowly, a nuisance, and those to be avoided, Christians saw Christ hidden within the poor, the widow, the orphan, and the beggar. Serving the poor is another way of serving Christ (Matt. 25). The Poor Laws change this worldview. When voluntary charity is replaced by state coercion, people slowly began to see the poor, not as Christ in disguise, but as a burden. The poor begin to be dehumanized.

One person who perceives the sting of the Poor Laws is an English cleric named Thomas Malthus (1766–1843). Malthus believes that the Poor Laws are actually increasing poverty. In his book, *An Essay on the Principle of Population* (1798), Malthus proposes that an increase in food production and distribution only temporarily increases the well-being of the populace, since the increase in well-being also increases human reproduction. A larger population consumes more food and erases whatever gains in well-being were originally enjoyed, whereupon some population-reducing event (war, famine, etc.) starts the cycle over again. This "oscillation," Malthus concludes, is part of human nature and can't be wiped away by State-enforced taxation. In fact, any attempt by the government to relieve the misery of the poor by redistributing wealth only worsens the lot of others, whether it's by driving up the price of food, driving down the price of labor, or hampering the "spirit of independence" among the peasantry.

Malthus therefore longs to rescind the Poor Laws. "The evil is perhaps too far to be remedied," he writes, "but I feel little doubt in my own mind that if the Poor Laws had never existed, though there might have been a few more instances of very severe distress, yet that the aggregate mass of happiness among the common people would have been much greater than it is at present."[160]

A great many thinkers over the ensuing generations will distort Malthus's work, caricaturing him as a crusader for reducing the population, by any means necessary, to prevent it from spinning out of control and ushering in global starvation. This gloss on Malthus must dehumanize the poor, segregating them from the rest of the human family. They will be found worthy, taking a few words from Malthus's essay, of suffering "severe distress" for the sake of the "aggregate mass of happiness."

The fear of mass starvation, with Malthus as a jumping-off point, will spawn many secular "end times preachers," who carry on the message and issue a multitude of failed predictions of doom, such as Paul Ehrlich's best-seller *The Population Bomb* (1970).[161]

HUMAN KNOWLEDGE
No-Popery Becomes Whig History

The fusion of State and Church, patriotism and piety, in England takes no-popery history to a new level. We saw earlier how the Magdeburg Centuriators attempted to provide a historical foundation for rejecting the historic Church. Protestant England builds on this edifice—only its goal is not to explain why the historic Church has fallen and needs a Protestant Reformation. Its goal is to justify its split with Rome, depress Catholic sympathies within the realm, and villainize England's foreign enemies. Something more is needed to galvanize the national consciousness and become part of its patriotic memory. The result is no-popery history.

The first book in this new strain is John Foxe's *Acts and Monuments of Christian Martyrs* (better known as *Foxe's Book of Martyrs*). The book chronicles with inflammatory rhetoric the death of Protestants at the hands of the bloody Catholic Church, especially during the brief reign of the Catholic Queen Mary I. The book essentially argues that Anglicanism is not an innovation, but the continuation of true Christians who were forever being hunted and killed by the Catholic Church. Foxe's book is an immensely popular and influential piece of nationalistic propaganda.

"Bloody" Mary, Bluff King Hal, and Good Queen Bess

This brand of history also shapes the way England looks at itself. Did you ever hear of *Bloody Mary*? The name refers to Mary I, the only child of Henry VIII and Catherine. Is her reign bloody? The best estimates put the death tolls as follows: King Henry VIII, between 57,000 and 72,000 deaths; Edward VI, about 5,000 deaths; Queen Mary, 284 deaths; and Elizabeth I at roughly the same as Mary. Even compensating for the different lengths of their reigns, Mary is no bloodier than any Protestant monarch, yet Mary is known as Bloody Mary, whereas Henry VIII and Elizabeth I are known by the monikers *Bluff King Hal* and *Good Queen Bess*. What makes Mary bloody? It isn't her cruelty or the number of people she executed. It's that she is a Catholic.

The Birth of the Black Legend

Another legend begins when the Catholic emperor Charles V's Spanish-imperial forces win a decisive victory over the Protestant forces at the Battle of Muhlberg in 1567. A propaganda campaign commences with the publication of a Protestant leaflet titled "A Discovery and Plaine Declaration of Sundry Subtill Practices of the Holy Inquisition of Spain," penned by Reginaldus Montanus, a supposed victim of the Spanish Inquisition. Montanus's work is a brilliant piece of propaganda, mixing truth with exaggerations, cherry-picking abuses so they seem to be the norm, and lionizing the victims as innocent collateral damage of Spanish Catholic zeal.

Whig History

When King Charles II's (1630–1685) younger brother James (1633–1701) becomes Catholic, another conflict emerges. The Whig party sees it in its best interest to use no-popery history to prevent England from having a Catholic monarch. The Dutch invasion of 1688 causes James to flee to the continent, while William of Orange becomes king. The Whig party now sits squarely in English politics. No-popery history becomes a tool to prevent the Jacobites (those who wish to restore James II to his rightful throne) from gaining a foothold in the conscience of English people. Whig history becomes the official history of the realm, and anyone who wishes to climb the ladder in British academia needs to toe the line.

Even after anti-Catholic polemics die down and new research comes to the fore, Whig history remains, shaping and distorting how the past is presented. As Hubert Butterfield (1900–1979) notes:

> But whether we take the context of Luther against the popes, or that of Philip II and Elizabeth . . . it appears that the historian tends in the first place to adopt the Whig or Protestant view of the subject, and very quickly busies himself with dividing the world into the friends and the enemies of progress. . . . This Whig tendency is so deep-rooted that even when piece-meal research has corrected the story in detail, we are slow in re-valuing the whole and reorganizing the broad outlines of the theme in light of these discoveries . . . that is, the tendency to patch the new research into the old story even when the research in detail has altered the bearings of the whole subject.[162]

According to this Whig configuration of history, "Protestants will be seen to have been fighting for the future, while it will be obvious that the Catholics were fighting for the past."[163] The common barb that Catholic teachings are "medieval" or "pre-scientific" is rooted in the myth created by Whig history.

If sanity is the degree to which what is known corresponds to what truly is, Whig history and no-popery history add more than a dash of insanity to our knowledge of the past and take us one step farther from reality.

IV.

EPISTEMOLOGICAL REVOLT

1632–1704	John Locke
1703–1758	Jonathan Edwards
1711–1776	David Hume
1712–1786	Frederick the Great
c. 1730–1755	First Great Awakening
c. 1790–1840	Second Great Awakening
1805–1844	Joseph Smith
1806–1873	John Stuart Mill
1809–1882	Charles Darwin
1879–1966	Margaret Sanger
1889–1945	Adolf Hitler
1891	The Unity church
1907	First eugenic sterilization law in the United States
1918–2018	Billy Graham
1942	Founding of Planned Parenthood

13

Inventing Religion

I esteem it above all things necessary
to distinguish exactly the business of civil
government from that of religion.

—JOHN LOCKE

Protestantism breaks into factions an astounding rate. A good example of its dissolution can be seen in controversies over the Eucharist. At the Marburg Colloquy in 1529, Zwingli and Luther cannot agree on the meaning of "this is my body." Forty-eight years later, in 1577, Christoph Rasperger is able to compile 200 different interpretations of the same words.[164]

Since Christendom is organized around State-Church governments, denominational divisions result in territorial divisions. Temporal rulers, charged with maintaining the peace and civil cogency through their use of the sword, use it in these religious disputes. Wars erupt between Catholics and Protestants, as well among different groups of Protestants.

Catholic and Protestant forces clashed in Switzerland in the late 1520s and early 1530s; Charles V defeated the

Schmalkaldic League in 1547 only to have his gains reversed before the stalemate of the Paces of Augsburg in 1555; French Huguenots and Catholics fought a bloody series of eight civil wars interspersed with religious riots between 1563 and 1598 with further hostilities lasting until 1629; the Dutch resisted Philip II's suppression of heresy beginning with the *Wonderjaar* of 1566, their revolt becoming, against William of Orange's wishes, a confessionalized struggle that endured off and on until 1648; the Thirty Years War, its battles and sieges situated mostly in central Europe, involved nearly all European countries at some point between 1618 and 1648; and in England, Puritan resistance to Charles I's "personal rule" led in the 1640s to two civil wars and widespread disruptions from which religion was inextricable.[165]

Little is accomplished through these conflicts. Confessional Protestantism (Lutheran and Reformed), which enjoys the backing of the State, succeeds to some extent in suppressing smaller splinter groups. But as far as restoring Protestants to the Catholic Faith, the wars are a failure. Indeed, not only do they fail, but they make Protestants intransigent in their anti-Catholicism.

GOD AND CREATION
The Search for Unity of Belief

These religious conflicts over doctrine and practice make Christianity look as if it were little more than a set of propositions or ideas, not a visible society bound by love. One group holds to one set of doctrines. Another holds to a different set. Since the historic Faith has been rejected, all that is left is opinions.

In light of the seemingly endless and fruitless conflicts over doctrine, a new idea comes about: if doctrinal purity is the cause of divisions within Protestantism, perhaps doctrinal ambiguity will bring unity!

Blurring the Edges

Philip I (1504–1567), landgrave of Hesse, whom we met earlier when he took a second wife, appears to be the first temporal ruler who seeks shelter in the fuzzy middle. When confronted with the irreconcilable differences over the Eucharist, Philip proposes that in order to bring about an end to what seems to him to be tedious bickering, that doctrine should remain fuzzy enough so that all can accept it.[166]

At the heart of Philip's approach to unity is reductionism. It begins by reducing the Faith to a set of propositions. When a proposition is contested, the proposition is relegated to a lesser, non-essential category or sufficiently blurred so as to admit the widest possible acceptance. Reductionism effectively erases religious imperatives—like those mentioned earlier that generated important revolutions of thought— and deconstructs the Christian worldview. As more and more Protestants differ in how they interpret Scripture, larger portions of the Faith begin to be pushed to the blurry, non-essential category. The only question is where to draw the line. How much are Protestants willing to jettison to restore some semblance of unity?

Deism

The French humanist Guillaume Postel (1510–1581) is willing to push the envelope of reductionism to the extreme by positing sixty-seven propositions that all religions hold in common. Once all the externalities of these religions are rejected, Postel argues, there will no longer be any religious divisions.[167] Postel's anti-incarnational approach pushes all the external physical aspects of the Faith to the non-essential category, leaving the bare "essential" sixty-seven.

Later, Lord Herbert of Cherbury (1583–1648) is even more reductionistic, reducing the essential propositions down to five.[168] These core beliefs reflect what he calls a *religious instinct*, deeply embedded in everyone, that is obscured by the encrustations of rituals, creeds, and ecclesiastical laws and practices. As historian William Cavanaugh puts it:

> Any particular doctrines and rites that arise in positive religions are a dilution of the original purity of the natural instinct as it becomes weighed down by the body and the material world. At best, such additions to pure religion are beneficial exemplifications of the underlying universal religion.[169]

Lord Herbert's proposal urges all to step back into a pre-Christian age, which he romanticizes as exhibiting the *religious instinct* in all its purity. Herbert's fantasy about the purity of primitive religious instinct paves the way to postmodern romanticizing and idealization of primitive cultures and the subsequent inferiority complex about the Christian West.

The ultimate expression of blurring to promote unity is *deism*. Deists deny that God interacts with the world after its creation, rejecting all positive revelation, leaving only reason and intuition as our means for knowing the Creator. Newtonian physics seems to support the deistic view of God, since it casts the cosmos as a giant machine run by the laws of nature. Where the irrational party in Islam insisted that God directly causes everything and denied all secondary causes, deism proposes the opposite. Only secondary causes exist after creation. If the former is true, the world isn't real. If the latter is true, God is largely irrelevant.

The deistic project is a failure. Christians don't abandon their "superfluous externalities of rite and practice" to embrace the god of deism. Instead, deism became yet another division that claims that the essence of religion is interior, non-material, and separate from the political order.[170]

HUMAN INTERGRITY AND VALUE
Double Truth Revisited

Just as salvation involves both soul and body as well as faith and good works, the Christian life and society are interrelated. Religion (Latin, *religio*) originally meant a duty or an obligation that binds society, whether that society be a family, a city, a group of monks, or the state. According to

St. Thomas Aquinas, it is a virtue to be practiced under the heading of justice.[171]

> For Aquinas *religio* did not belong to a separate, "supernatural" realm of activity. . . . Medieval Christendom was a theopolitical whole. . . . Acts of governing well, in other words, are directed toward the same end toward which *religio* is directed, and the true *religio* is integral to good governing.[172]

In other words, the Christian faith is not restricted to saving souls; its principles and teachings are also beneficial and integral to society, ordering all activities to our final end: union with God. The integrity of Christian life is rooted in the Incarnation and Christ's union with his body, the Church:

> The organic image of the body of Christ was fused with a hierarchical ordering of estates. There was no part of Christendom that stood outside of the holistic, sacralized order.[173]

A new vision of society began to take shape in the 1600s and 1700s, where *religio* was redefined as pertaining only to the interior belief and worship of God *as distinct from* the rest of life (i.e., secular life).

The seeds for this development go back to Luther, who reduces justification to faith alone apart from love and his view of the *two kingdoms*. These lines of thought continue and develop further within Protestantism so that "the internal-external and belief-practice binaries were crucial to the continued formation of the religious-secular binary in the sixteenth century."[174]

Since Christianity has been reduced to doctrinal propositions, and the desire to maintain these propositions in all their purity inflames endless religious wars and conflicts, a new understanding of *religion* is invented. It serves as a catch-all term for whatever is outside public life. According to the new state of affairs, *religion* is to be a distinct and separate sphere of life, a kind of safe zone, from the earthly pursuits common to all.

Religion is defined along Protestant lines concerning personal interior beliefs and doctrines; the secular sphere concerns the external world of labor, property, government, and everything else. But what happens when a religious teaching contradicts the secular view?

Initially, the two spheres are not mutually exclusive. Religion influences secular society, and secular society supports religion in general. As these two spheres begin to be viewed in a more mutually exclusive manner and secularism predominates, Christians adopt something similar to the Latin Averroists' *double truth*, where an individual affirms something as true in the sphere of religion and also its contrary in secular society. We see the modern version of *double truth* today when people are said to be "personally opposed to abortion," but in public life, they advocate for it.

Cultural Momentum

The religious–secular truth dichotomy gains wide acceptance because it seems to work. The sky doesn't fall overnight. Life continues under the new system. What people fail to recognize is that over the centuries before this change, the Church had sustained a kind of cultural momentum. For a long time, all people in Western society shared to varying degrees the same worldview. But as Protestantism fractures and secularism predominates, cultural inertia sets in and begins to grow.

If the truths of the Faith have no real application to the external world, what is the Faith? As Thomas Aquinas complained against the Latin Averroists, the Faith is reduced to a *position*. Even worse, the religious–secular binary reverses the revolutions of thought caused by the Incarnation. Supernatural charity cannot be exercised as a personal interior belief, nor can one believe that women and children are persons with intrinsic dignity and not expect society to do the same. Like the serpent's lie, the assumption is that God can reveal something as true that isn't necessarily good or beneficial. The invention of *religion* effectively cuts the Western world off from the source that brought it about and sustained it.

THE CHURCH
Reaction to Miracles

Earlier, we saw how the historic fact of the visible identifiable Church persisting through the centuries from the time of

Christ to the Reformation posed a serious obstacle for the legitimacy of the Protestant revolt. Protestantism responded with a reconfigured and sometimes fictitious counter-history beginning with the Centuriators and evolving into Whig history.

Nor is history the only aspect of the Church that needs to be confronted. At the Reformation, Catholics also appeal to the ongoing abundance of miracles in the Church as a sign of its divine origin (John 14:12). The combination of history and the appeal to miracles presents a formidable apologetic for the Church.

Luther, Calvin, and others react to this claim by denying the continuance of miracles after the first generation of Christians. They grant that God initially performed miracles to confirm the gospel message and grow the Church, but then miracles largely ceased. As theologian Craig Keener explains:

Luther and especially Bucer blamed Catholic miracles on the devil, and later Protestants carried this reproach even further. The Reformers' antisupernaturalism, never adopted by Roman Catholic or Eastern Orthodox Christians, served their immediate polemical situation against Catholic apologetic use of miracle claims. Early Protestants sought to discredit medieval miracles, for the most part wholesale; while critical inquiry might have proved more helpful, the reaction against miracles associated with the traditional Roman Church was predominantly polemical.[175]

Denying ongoing miracles places Protestantism on the same ground as an unbelieving skeptic. All modern miracle claims must be false, since miracles had ceased in the first Christian centuries. This argument also aids in branding pious Catholics who look for God's intervention as superstitious, gullible people.

The denial of ongoing miracles has far-reaching and disastrous consequences for Christianity. Miracles are an extension of the Incarnation in that nearly all of them— with exceptions, such as the conversion of Saul—occur along with some sort of physical medium, whether it be the spoken word, the presence of a holy person, or contact with a relic or other item. The anti-miraculous stance within Protestantism fits well with its corresponding anti-sacramental movements.

Even worse, the cessation idea cleaves time into two eras: one where God acted robustly and in a public fashion in the past and the later era, where God works only invisibly and spiritually within the believer's heart. This allows, as Keener explains, the Reformers to affirm the truth of biblical miracles while denying the miracles of "the papists":

Developing the magisterial Reformers' reaction against abuses, some Protestants eventually selectively adopted the dogmatic antisupernaturalism of the radical Enlightenment. . . . It proved convenient for them to embrace thoroughgoing naturalism in the present era, in order to reject the miracle claims of "papists" and "enthusiasts" while excepting those recounted in Scripture. Belief that miracles had ceased offered a way to accommodate belief in biblical miracles with a current "orderly and rational universe," though it could never ultimately satisfy a uniformitarianism that demanded the same hegemony of natural law in the past.

The line drawn by Protestants between a period when miracles happened and when they don't happen not only appears to be *ad hoc* and arbitrary, but also ultimately undermines the credibility of biblical miracles. Certainly, if miracles could be rejected and discounted in the latter age, what would prevent someone from asserting the same lack of credibility in the former age? Why exclude the New Testament from skepticism?

A similar thing occurred with the Old Testament canon. After Luther's rejection of certain books of the Bible as *apocrypha*, Protestants argue that those books cannot be inspired Scripture since they contain supposed contradictions, errors, magic, and other difficulties. Once this line of criticism is accepted in principle, there is no reason why the same criticism can't be used against the protocanonical books of the Old *and* New Testaments. As the Lutheran theologian Edward Ruess (1804–1891) notes, "the scoffs thrown at the little fish of Tobit will sooner or later destroy Jonah's whale."[176]

Indeed, it is the dogmatic denial of the existence of modern Christian miracles that fuels and lends credibility to David Hume's argument against the possibility of all miracles.[177]

COMMUNITY
Acquisitiveness

Originally, the Dutch Republic is just as divided on religion as any other area. Religious toleration does evolve, but in a haphazard and complex way.[178] However, the resolve of secular rulers to enforce the established church, such as it is, is weak, and authorities are far more concerned with commerce and other earthly pursuits. With the shift in priorities from heavenly wealth to earthly goods, the Christian emphasis on worldly detachment and simple living erodes and is replaced with acquisitiveness, a strong desire for acquiring or possessing goods and wealth. The Dutch Republic finds itself in the unique position to answer this newfound demand.[179]

By the seventeenth century, the Dutch Republic reaches its zenith, a golden age, with its extensive trade, science, military, and art. Its worldly success becomes the envy of Europe, sparking international competition for the acquisition of more wealth, more trade, and more material goods. The switch from heavenly concerns to the earthly acquisition of material goods may suppress religious conflicts, but it lays the groundwork for future worldwide conflicts of secular nation-states and the rampant consumerism now seen in the West.

GOVERNMENT
Secular Unity Versus Religious Unity

The most influential figure to promote the religion-state dichotomy is the philosopher John Locke (1632–1704). Locke endeavors to erect an immovable wall between these two spheres:

I esteem it above all things necessary to distinguish exactly the business of civil government from that of religion, and to settle the just bounds that lie between one and the other. If this be not done, there can be no end put to the controversies that will be always arising between those that have, or at least pretend to have, on the one side, a concernment for the interest of men's souls, and, on the other side, a care for the commonwealth.

The commonwealth seems to me to be a society of men constituted only for the procuring, preserving, and advancing their own civil interests.

Civil interests I call life, liberty, health, and indulgency of body; and the possession of outward things, such as money, lands, houses, furniture, and the like.[180]

Locke views religious belief as something not anchored in reality, but rather only a predilection of the mind—a private interior matter. Because of this misconception, the supposed boundaries he erected to distinguish *religion* from the commonwealth are not as impregnable as he supposes. Locke's short list of civil interests contains a few important items that are just as much "religious" as they are secular. Take *life* as an example. What is life? When does it begin? Is human life property? Under what circumstances can life justly end? All these are religious and philosophical questions, not secular. The same is true for liberty—is it the freedom to do what one ought, or is it the freedom to do whatever one desires?

These questions are so fundamental that they are outside the competency of secular governments to determine. And yet, according to Locke's perspective, *religion* has no control or authority over these *civil interests*.

The contrast with the medieval Christian context is sharp. The idea that a "religious society" has no say over how civil and worldly goods are handled would be entirely foreign not only to the craft guilds whose work revolved around the liturgy, but also to the monastic communities whose vows were not merely a dispossession of all concern for worldly goods, but a recognition that the religious life is intimately entwined with how one interacts with such goods.[181]

Locke writes:

The church itself is a thing absolutely separate and distinct from the commonwealth. The boundaries on both sides are fixed and immovable. He jumbles heaven and earth together, the things most remote and opposite, who mixes these two societies, which are, in their original, end, business, and in everything perfectly distinct and infinitely different from one another.[182]

In effect, Locke is not distinguishing the two orders of government, but annexing and dispossessing things that were formerly under the State-Church and ceding them to the sphere of civil government. We already saw this usurpation taking place piecemeal, such as when rulers altered the nature of marriage for the sake of political expediency.

With the Incarnation and the unity of Christ in head and body, heaven and earth are joined. The eternal works within the temporal, the infinite with the finite, the incorruptible with the corruptible. Death becomes the means to life. God became man so that by being united to Christ, man should partake of the divine nature and be a member of Christ's body, the Church. We creatures are ennobled in such a way as to lift our fallen humanity to unbelievable new heights. Locke's proposal—which replaces the old order—separates what God had joined together in Christ and exiles the divine and heavenly elements into a hermetically sealed private realm.

We can love one another as Christ loved us as long as doing so doesn't transgress the "fixed and immovable" boundary of the secular sphere. But isn't feeding the poor a type of commerce and exchange of goods? Isn't the care of the downtrodden more than a purely interior disposition of the soul? Acts of love are just as much external, physical, material as they are internal. Christianity simply doesn't fit into this secular-religious dichotomy. As Cavanaugh points out:

> The very claim that the boundaries between religion and nonreligion are natural, eternal, fixed, and immutable is *itself* a part of the new configuration of power that comes about with the rise of the modern state. The new state's claim to a monopoly on violence, lawmaking, and public

allegiance within a given territory depends upon either the absorption of the Church into the State or the relegation of the church to an essentially private realm.[183]

The State is now free to do whatever it willed without the capping power of the Church. To transform the State in line with the gospel would be to transgress the "fixed and immovable" boundary separating the two.

No Capping Authority

The twentieth century provides us with several examples of how this self-imposed boundary is used as a weapon to remove any cap on government authority. For example, Germany's National Socialists (Nazis) used this dichotomy to silence the Church's criticism of their brutal regime. As Adolf Hitler said in a speech made on September 11, 1935:

> Today it is we who have this power; and we shall never wage the war as a war against Christianity or even against one of the two denominations; but we shall wage it in order to keep our public life free from those priests who have fallen short of their calling, and *who think they have to be politicians*, not pastors of the flock.[184]

Not only does the Church lose its ability to limit what governments can morally do, but governments can use the "fixed and immovable boundaries" idea to delegitimize Christian views from forming and informing the secular sphere.

HUMAN KNOWLEDGE
Science and Its Goals

The Christian motivation to understand nature is to learn about God's wisdom in creating and sustaining it. However, this motive is overshadowed by a new and stronger motivation for the pursuit of profitability and to satisfy acquisitiveness. As historian Brad Gregory points out:

> Harold Cook has shown the extent to which the early modern Dutch ambition to discover, describe, and classify natural objects throughout the world was driven by commercial interests, the desire for profit, and "warm hope of material progress and gain more than otherworldly aestheticism": inquisitiveness was propelled by acquisitiveness.[185]

This is not to suggest that the pursuit of knowledge is always for the sake of the common good or purely out of the love to learn more. It isn't. Once the secular world is unplugged from religion, acquisitiveness bends the focus of scientific research from the pursuit of knowledge of God in creation to those things that have the greatest potential for profit.

Undirected Nature

David Hume (1711–1776), one of the most influential Enlightenment philosophers, denies that man has any innate knowledge (i.e., reason) and argues that man's sole means of knowledge is experience. For him, things like inductive reasoning and causality cannot be rationally established; rather, they are simply a codification of things we habitually experience. Cause and effect, according to his view, are really "loose and separate" items.

It's not difficult to see that Hume's critique, although operating on different premises, fits well within the nominalist conception of God, whose will is unconstrained, even by reason, although he customarily acts in certain ways. With the rational basis for efficient causality erased, the goal-directedness of things—the final causality or teleology—disappears. All that remains is people's impressions of things that habitually happen in a certain way.

Hume uses experience to deny miracles. Since miracles are rare and the laws of nature are based on regularity, miracles are impossible, because either they violate the laws of nature or they are based on the weak evidence of personal testimony. Hume's argument is made plausible by the Protestant claim that miracles ceased over a millennium ago. Since miracles are part of a bygone age and supported only by human testimony, Hume disbelieves that anything—including biblical miracles—can overturn what we experience with natural laws.

As philosopher Edward Feser notes, there is a basic incoherence in Hume's overall philosophy. When it comes to his views on causality, he permits irregularities within nature, but when it comes to miracles, suddenly, the law of nature become ironclad.[186]

Scientific Specialization

The denial of final causes or teleology in science changes the whole enterprise. Where science had once attempted to integrate knowledge into a coherent whole, it becomes specialized and compartmentalized. As a result, we learn more and more about less and less. Science, like everything else affected by the nominalist worldview, becomes atomized.[187]

14

Retreat from Reality

Every feeble-minded girl or woman
of the hereditary type, especially of the
moron class, should be segregated during
the reproductive period.

—MARGARET SANGER

Our next epoch marks a remarkable retreat from reality and the Incarnation—but to where? The only place to retreat is to our interior life and introspection.

GOD AND CREATION

How Do We Know We Are the Elect?

Calvinism raised the question: how do we know we are the elect? Calvin believed that one's assurance of election is found through participation in rightly ordered worship, in the ministry of the word, and in the sacraments.

But what about Calvinists who could not access Calvin's rightly ordered worship and sacraments? This is the predicament English Puritanism faces after it fails to reform the

English church along Calvinistic lines. If participating in rightly ordered worship is not possible, there must be some other means to determine one's election.

The solution is introspection. Through self-contemplation, people look for interior signs that they're predestined to glory. But what are these signs? Different Puritans list different signs.[188] The most famous of these are Jonathan Edward's (1703–1758) twelve *marks* of affectional attachment to God.[189]

Introspection begins to affect how people understood *the church*, especially among separatist Puritans in New England:

> The Calvinists of New England drew out the ecclesial consequences of this new emphasis on interior experience and assurance. Puritan separatists sought to overcome their exclusion from the national church by "covenanting" with fellow "saints" to form autonomous congregations. . . . The insistence on assurance and interiority did not immediately destroy either objective church polity or morality, but the seeds were sown.[190]

The New England Puritans are the most influential religious group within the colonial United States; their changes and innovations affect the outlook of the whole nation.[191]

THE CHURCH

Conversionism

The Puritan project attempts to hold together theology, society, and individuals through covenants. Regeneration becomes the prerequisite for church membership and partaking of the Lord's Supper. This doesn't please everyone, especially those who are excluded. Opposition to the "unscriptural" system comes with counter-proposals on how the nation can be considered part of a covenant and all can participate in it. In the end, the Puritan synthesis simply collapsed.[192]

Edwards and his co-laborer and revivalist George Whitefield (1714–1770) will propose a new, radically reductionistic view of faith called *conversionism*. Under this view, the conversion experience becomes the bottom line for one's knowledge of election and salvation. Church membership is rendered meaningless. As Whitefield says:

> I saw regenerate souls among the Baptists, among the Presbyterians, among the Independents, and among the Church [i.e., Anglican] folks—all children of God, and yet all born again in a different way of worship: and who can tell which is the most evangelical? . . . It was best to preach the new birth, and the power of godliness, and not to insist so much on the form: for people would never be brought to one mind as to that; nor did Jesus Christ ever intend it.[193]

As David Anders notes:

> By making the marks of regeneration essentially interior ("religious affections") rather than sacramental, he prepared the way for a radical, redefinition of "true church."

Whitefield's denominationalism now follows logically. The true church is simply the one containing all those possessing the (self-attested) interior marks of regeneration.[194]

Conversionism seems to circumvent the problem of doctrinal sectarianism and the drive for doctrinal purity. No longer will participating in rightly ordered worship, church membership, profession of creeds, sacraments, or even believing in the gospel serve as a sign of election. Everything is reduced to a conversion experience. Once you've experienced it, you're a member of the true church, regardless of what you believe, where you worship, or what religious group you belong to.

Conversionism lights the fire of the *Second Great Awakening* that spreads across young America. Evangelists of all stripes ride out to the countryside and cities, holding revival meetings, to bring this experience about. Charles Granderson Finney (1792-1875), a revivalist during the period, "defended the idea that regeneration is something that can be chosen and effected immediately and entirely through mental processes."[195] Revival meetings are designed to provoke a powerful emotional response that will be interpreted as manifesting the signs of regeneration. What are these signs? Some people throw themselves to the ground and rise up dancing. Others bark like dogs. Still others walk about in a trance-like state. There are bursts of crying, laughing, speaking in tongues, and other ecstatic phenomena.

After the revival meetings, where do those who have a conversion experience go? Many go to the denomination of the preacher. A Calvinist minister holds a revival and points people to a local Calvinist church. A Baptist preacher points to the local Baptist church, and so on. In this way, the Second Great Awakening brings rural Protestants face to face with the scandal of Protestant sectarianism. It also raises these questions: "Which one is right?" "Is any of them right?"

The emotion-driven enthusiasm of conversionism takes its toll. There is no doubt that many of these conversions are real and sincere. However, once the euphoria of the conversion experience vanishes, something has to take its place.

The Restoration Movement

The Second Great Awakening generates numerous movements to fill in that gap and provide a solution to Protestant disunity. Several of these movements fall under the umbrella term of *restoration movements*. If Christianity is to be restored to its original purity and unity, there needs to be either new extra-biblical revelation or a more vigorous form of *sola scriptura* (the Bible alone).

Mormonism

Joseph Smith, Jr. (1805–1844), the founder of Mormonism, claims that after attending a revival meeting, he went off to pray about which church to join. He says God appeared to him, telling him all are wrong and that God was going to restore his church through Smith. Smith's "revelations" provide divine answers to all the most heated questions of the day, along with the Book of Mormon that he "discovers" buried near his property. Like the Münster prophets, Smith reinstitutes polygamy, even with women already married. Ultimately, Mormonism too splinters into various sects, each claiming to be the true restored church.

Adventism

In the wake of the rush of religious enthusiasm generated by the Second Great Awaking, William Miller (1782–1849) causes a new sensation when he propounds that the Bible teaches that Christ's Second Coming is going to happen between 1843 and 1844. The Millerites set out preaching and fan religious fervor as 1844 approaches. When nothing happens, the movement collapses amid tremendous emotional and financial devastation.[196]

A sizable segment of Millerites, however, see *the Great Disappointment* as a divine test of their faith. A self-proclaimed prophetess, Ellen Gould White (1827–1915), claims that Miller's computation was correct, but what it was meant to predict was wrong. The date foretells not the Second Coming, but rather the heavenly cleansing of the temple and the beginning of God's *investigative judgment*.[197] White travels the country, asserting that Sabbath Day worship is the mark of true Christians and that at the end of time, the Catholic Church will martyr all Sabbath-keeping Christians. Her followers are known today as the *Seventh-day Adventists*.

There are other Adventist sects as well. Perhaps the best known today are the Christadelphians and the Jehovah's Witnesses.

Spiritism and Mind Science

American spiritism also fills the emotional and experiential void left by the Second Great Awakening. In 1848, the Fox sisters of Hydesville, New York convince their parents and neighbors that they can communicate with spirits. Consulting spirit guides, departed loved ones, and a host of other spiritual entities becomes all the rage. Others, such as Emanuel Swedenborg (1688–1772) and Franz Mesmer (1734–1815), also had contributed to the quest to seek knowledge about the afterlife. By 1867, nearly a third of the United States is involved in one way or another with *spiritism*.[198] Spiritism becomes systematized under the influence of occultist Helena Blavatsky (1831–1891), co-founder of the Theosophical Society, which claims to be "a synthesis of science, religion, and philosophy."

Charles (1854–1948) and Myrtle Fillmore (1845–1931), who believe that spiritual healing cured Myrtle's tuberculosis, begin studying world religions, spiritual healings, and related subjects. In 1891, they form the Unity church. Unity, like deism, seeks to unify mankind under a set of universal beliefs, only Unity's beliefs are pantheistic (all is God); *monistic* (everything is one); and Gnostic, since "salvation" comes about through introspection and self-awareness.

Unity's description of the church sounds remarkably like that of Protestant conversionism:

The church of God [is] its activity in man as a mental perception. . . . In its outer sense the church of Christ consists of all persons in whom the consciousness of Truth has become firmly established; whether or not they belong to a denominational church makes no difference. They comprise the great brotherhood which Jesus Christ established in Spirit. The true church is not made of creed and forms . . . the heart of man is its temple and the Spirit of truth is the one guide into all Truth. When men learn to turn within to the Spirit of truth, who is in each one for his light and inspiration, the difference between the churches of man will be eliminated, and the one church will be recognized.[199]

The Unity church will become influential in the late 1900s with the generation of a fantasy-based view of reality known as the New Age Movement.

Patternism

Not every restorationist group seeks extra-biblical revelation. The Stone–Campbell movement, for example, goes to the other extreme by setting aside all creeds, confessions, and doctrines in order to to reconstruct primitive Christianity from the pages of the New Testament as if it were a biblical design or *pattern* for the church. Once the pattern is deciphered and established, all will see the biblical purity of the restored church and join. The result, however, is yet another Protestant sect that will splinter into sects of its own.

Malthus, Darwin, and the Final Solution

Charles Darwin's (1809–1882) theory of evolution and natural selection offers secularists hope for a science-based alternative to the Christian worldview. Evolution offers a naturalistic teleology, where species are ordered not to their final end—a cosmos manifesting God's wisdom—but toward survival and propagation.

Can Darwinism be used to order society and morality just as Christian teleology once did? Darwin considers the possibility when he contrasts how we care for the poor:

> With savages, the weak in body or mind are soon eliminated; and those that survive commonly exhibit a vigorous state of health. We civilized men, on the other hand, do our utmost to check the process of elimination; we build asylums for the imbecile, the maimed, and the sick; we institute poor-laws; and our medical men exert their utmost skill to save the life of every one to the last moment. . . . Thus the weak members of civilized societies propagate their kind. *No one who has attended to the breeding of domestic animals will doubt that this must be highly injurious to the race of man.* It is surprising how soon a want of care, or care wrongly directed, leads to the degeneration of a domestic race; but excepting in the case of man himself, hardly any one is so ignorant as to allow his worst animals to breed.[200]

What's curious is what he says afterward:

The aid which we feel impelled to give to the helpless is mainly an *incidental result* of the *instinct of sympathy*, which was originally acquired as part of the social instincts, but subsequently rendered, in the manner previously indicated, more tender and more widely diffused. Nor could we check our sympathy, even at the urging of hard reason, without deterioration in the noblest part of our nature.[201]

Darwin exhibits a certain historical amnesia when he speaks about how "instinctive" it is for us to care for the less fortunate. Apparently, the ancient world had some sort of genetic blocker that inhibits this "instinct" from being realized. What Darwin identifies as an incidental "instinct" is the cultural momentum instilled by centuries of Catholicism, which so revolutionized human thought in the West that the charity it promotes could be mistaken for a natural instinct.

Ethical Darwinism and Eugenics

Sir Francis Galton (1822–1911) takes Darwin's insight one step farther and becomes the *father of eugenics*. In the early 1900s, eugenics is seen as cutting-edge thought in human health and development. It pushes back against Darwin's noble instinct and uses the coercive power of the State to limit undesirables by the restriction of marriage and even compulsory sterilization. As shocking as it may seem, the

United States backs forced sterilization. After all, it is scientific! Indiana in 1907 becomes the first state to force individuals to be sterilized, and more than thirty states follow. The U.S. Supreme Court in 1927 upholds as constitutional a Virginia law allowing for the compulsory sterilization of patients of state mental institutions.

Eugenics is promoted through the American Birth Control League, established by Margaret Sanger (1879–1966) in 1921. In 1942, the League changes its name to Planned Parenthood Federation of America. Its aim is published in its *Birth Control Review*:

> To promote eugenic birth selection throughout the United States so that there may be more well-born and fewer ill-born children—a stronger, healthier and more intelligent race.[202]

Sanger's *Pivot of Civilization* states:

> There is every indication that feeble-mindedness in its protean forms is on the increase, that it has leaped the barriers, and that there is truly, as some of the scientific eugenists have pointed out, a feeble-minded peril to future generations—unless the feeble-minded are prevented from reproducing their kind. . . . Every feeble-minded girl or woman of the hereditary type, especially of the moron class, should be segregated during the reproductive period. Otherwise, she is almost certain to

bear imbecile children, who in turn are just as certain to breed other defectives.[203]

Sanger's words echo the by now longstanding popular take on the work of Thomas Malthus, only Malthus's concern was poverty. Sanger's concern is runaway "defectives" who will cripple the future. But what makes an individual "feeble-minded" or "defective"? Sanger speaks as if such people can be identified by established clinical benchmarks. But later in the same work, she writes:

> Are we to check the infant mortality rate among the feeble-minded and aid the unfortunate offspring to grow up a menace to the civilized community *even when not actually certifiable as mentally defective or not obviously imbecile?*[204]

Sanger's subjectivism is dangerous. Who determines whether someone is "feeble-minded"? Who determines whether someone is a "menace to society"?

Notice also how Sanger excludes the "feeble-minded" from the "civilized community." She (or the eugenicist) determines whether one is "feeble-minded." She becomes the judge of who is to be excluded from the human family.

Historic Christianity affirmed the dignity of each human as being rooted in what it is: a human being made in the image and likeness of God. Here, human value is measured by what it does—whether people can contribute to society.

Eugenics is an international concern. In 1933, Sanger's magazine reprints an article written for its English readers, titled "Eugenic Sterilization," by Ernst Rudin, the chief architect of the Nazi sterilization program and founder of the *Gesellschaft fur Rassenhygiene* (Society for Racial Hygiene).[205]

Nazis and Eugenics

During the same year, the Nazi government passes the Law for the Prevention of Progeny with Hereditary Diseases. Its goal (and the goal of others like it) is to purge German society and its territories of undesirables to breed a pure Aryan society. It calls for the sterilization of all persons who suffer from mental illness, physical deformity, feeble-mindedness, learning disabilities, epilepsy, blindness, deafness, and severe alcoholism. All of these things, according to the science of the day, are hereditary diseases.

But who or what determines whether a person suffers from a mental illness or a learning disability? The government does. What if a person believes that National Socialism is evil? Does he suffer from a mental illness or feeble-mindedness? Moreover, why stop at sterilization? Aren't these people still a drain on society? It is the State that decides, and the State is limited only by what it is willing to do. The National Socialist government is prepared to do whatever is necessary to achieve its national goals.

After this act, the Nazis ramp up their propaganda against the disabled, referring to them as "life unworthy of life."

According to the American Holocaust Museum's article "People with Disabilities":

> In the autumn of 1939, Adolf Hitler secretly authorized a medically administered program of "mercy death" code-named "Operation T4." . . . Between 1940 and 1941 approximately 70,000 Austrian and German disabled people were killed under the T4 program, most via large-scale killing operations using poison gas. (This methodology served as the precursor to the streamlined extermination methods of the "Final Solution.") Although Hitler formally ordered a halt to the program in late August 1941, the killings secretly continued until the war's end, resulting in the murder of an estimated 275,000 people with disabilities.[206]

When the Nazi leadership are put on trial at Nuremberg after World War Two, they try to justify their sterilization program—which sterilized nearly a half a million people in less than a decade—by pointing to the United States as their inspiration.

HUMAN KNOWLEDGE
Conflict and the Conflict Myth

In the late 1800s, nominal Protestants and unbelievers develop a new no-popery myth. Building on Whig history, which presents all things Catholic as backward, unenlightened, and regressive, it proposes that Catholicism is at war with science.

The genesis of this myth can be traced to two influential books: John W. Draper's *The Conflict Between Science and Religion* (1874) and the two-volume work *A History of the Warfare of Science with Theology in Christendom* (1896) by Andrew Dixon White, the first president of Cornell University.

According to Draper, the supposed conflict "commenced when Christianity began to attain political power."[207] By this he means Catholicism. More specifically, "dogmatic Christianity" is the bad guy, since

> a divine revelation must necessarily be intolerant of contradiction; it must repudiate all improvement in itself, and view with disdain that arising from the progressive intellectual development of man.[208]

Draper's book is a mix of old no-popery canards and ill founded claims, such as that the Church once believed that the earth is flat. However, it is Andrew Dixon White's *tour de force* that proves more influential by masking its anti-religious propaganda under a veneer of scholarly acumen.

White's work is motivated by his visceral reaction to his own religious higher education. He abolishes any kind of religious test for faculty and students at Cornell, making the university, as he puts it, "an asylum for Science—where truth shall be sought for truth's sake, not stretched or cut exactly to fit Revealed Religion."[209] Like Draper's work, White's *History* brims with unfounded, ill founded, and just plain incorrect assertions. Like all no-popery works, it's one-sided and simplistic.

Draper's and White's books mark a transition in Whig history—from the no-popery myths that Protestants use against Catholicism to a secular apologetic against all "dogmatic Christianity."

Darwinism and Creationism

One wonders if the conflict myth would have survived had it not been for the general reaction of some Protestants and Catholics against Darwinism. Although the topic is too complex to address here, it is enough to say Catholics have less of a problem with a theistic version of Darwinism than conservative Protestants. For Catholics, some elements within the theory of evolution, such as chance, mutation, and secondary causation, can be reconciled with divine Providence.[210] Indeed, St. Thomas Aquinas dealt with these issues centuries before Darwin.[211] Catholics object to evolution in other areas, such as issues concerning some atheistic versions of the theory, causality, essences, and the science behind it.

Protestantism is different. It tends to de-emphasize secondary causes, a trait that can be traced back to Calvin and nominalism.[212] This tendency to see God working directly in creation makes the prospect of the special creation of each species more attractive, especially for Fundamentalist Protestants' literalistic reading of Genesis 1–2. When conflicts over this subject make headlines, the public cannot distinguish between Protestant Fundamentalist objections and those of other groups, so they wrongly paint Christianity as a whole as being anti-science.

15

Christianity Becomes an Idea

Faith in Jesus Christ saves you,

not faith in the Church.

—BILLY SUNDAY

By the second half of the twentieth century, the cultural momentum of Christendom has waned, and the ever-increasing atomization caused by nominalism has pushed more and more "essential" doctrines and practices into the "non-essential" category in order to maintain some sort of unity.

GOD AND CREATION

Conversionism and Gnosis

Conservative Protestantism, especially in America, is undergoing a conversionistic revolution of its own. Earlier, we saw how Charles Finney equated regeneration with "a change in the disposition of the mind."[213] Not everyone agrees with Finney. Quite a few don't. Nevertheless, conversionism gains a large following within Protestant Evangelicalism, eventually becoming formalized and reduced to a simple process, beginning with D.L. Moody (1837–1899), Billy Graham (1918–2018) in his book *Peace with God*, and Bill Bright (1921–2003)'s discussion of *The Four Spiritual Laws*.[214]

Faith is no longer the supernatural gift in which we assent to the whole truth as revealed by God through his Church. Rather, it is a reflexive faith, a change in the disposition of the mind—Christ's salvific work is done *for me*. Conversionism reduces faith to a kind of gnosis and salvation to an interior personal relationship.

A personal relationship with God is certainly a good thing. It would be tragic if a Christian didn't enjoy intimate friendship with God. But we can have a personal relationship with many people—parents, co-workers, next-door neighbors, even people we have met only online. As close as these relationships may be, they are not equal. Your flesh-and-blood relationship with your parents and the one-flesh union with your spouse are categorically different. The same is true for our union with Christ: we become his body and bride through faith and the sacraments, especially baptism and the Eucharist. This is why Catholics in the past rarely used "personal relationship" language. Instead, they spoke of being a devoted son or daughter.

HUMAN INTEGRITY AND VALUE
Rejecting the Dead and Dying

Our union in Christ and with each other binds us in such a way that even death cannot separate us. In this communion, things like hospitals, charitable works, offering prayers, Masses for the dead, honoring the saints, and proper burial are all interconnected. All are systematically dismantled by Protestantism and subsequent revolutions. Slowly, death is once again pushed outside the city.

Multi-generation households were common not long ago. Children were exposed to the whole of human experience: their mother giving birth to siblings, adolescence, adulthood, old age, and finally death. When someone died, his body lay in state in the home and was buried at the church cemetery. Funeral homes replace this practice. Next come retirement homes and hospices. These are not bad things, but they do remove the elderly and death from our common experience—and, in a way, exclude them from our community.

Expensive funerals have forced many to find alternatives to burials, often depriving family and friends of the chance to view their loved ones one last time. Experiencing death gives life a kind of sobriety; it reminds us that we need to use our limited time on earth wisely. It also sharpens our faith in the bodily resurrection, which saves us from despair. All this has been taken away from us.

The intuitive notion that our loved ones survive death and our natural desire to be reunited with them take a particularly gruesome secular expression when society replaces the communion of saints with its own products. Instead of prayers and Masses, people now wear jewelry that contains the cremated remains of their loved ones. People even have themselves tattooed with ink mixed with a loved one's ashes. The modern world's understanding of life and death, holiness and love, has become distorted.

Marriage Becomes Secularized

Marriage suffered through numerous revolts up to this point, most attacking its indissolubility and transferring its regulation from the Church to the State. Luther, for example, recognized matrimony not as a sacrament, but as something to be regulated by temporal rulers.[215] Likewise, some Protestants claimed that a lawful marriage could be dissolved after adultery or willful desertion.[216]

Although Protestants generally do not consider matrimony a sacrament, they do believe it to be a solemn contract. If one party wishes to divorce, there will be repercussions, just as there are penalties for breaking a secular contract. But eventually, even this idea comes under attack.

The first assault comes from the Prussian Calvinist turned skeptic Frederick the Great (1712–1786), who issues an edict in 1757 that childless marriages can be dissolved without guilt being imposed upon either spouse. The edict is incorporated into the General Laws of the Prussian State and becomes the first no-fault divorce law. Later, during the anti-Catholic *Kulturkampf* campaign under Bismarck in 1874, a new marriage law is passed that divests priests of their oversight over marriage and requires all German couples to first engage in a civil marriage before being married in the Church. In December 1917, Communist Russia likewise divests the Russian Orthodox Church of its jurisdiction and bestows authority on state offices to grant divorces.

The Rise of Biblical Experts

Just as the restoration movements attempt to restore Christianity back to its primitive purity, *critical biblical scholarship* attempts to do the same with the New Testament. Its hermeneutical suspicion is merely the extension of the same suspicion of the Church instilled by the Reformers. Only it is not the medieval Church or even the early Church that is presumed guilty until proven innocent; now it is the first-generation Church. Through critical studies, these scholars hope to "restore" (or rather reduce) the New Testament to its primitive purity by removing what they believe are later traditions and proto-Catholic encrustations. The result is an atomization and a reductionistic view of the sacred text.

The Law of Moses is not a compilation given by God to Moses, but a patchwork of different sources from varying perspectives stitched together by an unknown editor or editors. Likewise, the Gospels are reduced to bits and pieces of genuine sayings of the Lord surrounded by later material.

This fundamental distrust of the historic Christian witness leads to the distinction between *the Christ of faith* and *the historic Jesus*. The result isn't the discovery of new and genuine knowledge, but a reduction of true knowledge.

The rise of *Higher Criticism* also reorders how Protestants approach Scripture. No longer is the study and exposition of Scripture the exclusive domain of the clergy; it is now the exclusive domain of "the experts." Clergy who wish to know the truth about the sacred texts need to learn it through these specialists. The study of Scripture, like other fields affected by latent nominalism, has become compartmentalized, specialized, and the special domain of *the knowing ones*.

Lowest Common Denominationalism

When a *conversion experience* becomes the lowest common denominator that unites all Christians, the church community can, itself, be viewed as an impediment to unity. As David Anders notes:

> In its most extreme form, this evangelical ecclesiology devolves into popular rants against any church. This is not new. We find essentially the same thing in the well-known revivalist Billy Sunday (1862–1935): "Jesus said: 'Come to me,' not to the Church; to me, not to a creed; to me, not to a preacher; to me, not to an evangelist; to me, not to a priest; to me, not to a pope; 'Come to me and I will give you rest.' Faith in Jesus Christ saves you, not faith in the Church."[217]

Where the magisterial Protestants see church membership and rightly ordered worship as essential to the Christian life, conversionism places all those things in competition with Christ. All churches, in this view, are the same. For the believer, they all are either inconsequential or impediments and distractions that insinuate themselves between the believer and Christ.

Non-Denominationalism

As conversionism spreads, denominations and denominational labels soon become unpopular. Thus is born a new phenomenon: *non-denominationalism*. What is non-denominationalism? It is a Protestant denomination that doesn't want to be called a denomination. Non-denominationalists' beliefs generally mirror that of the Baptist faith; they are low-church, Bible-alone, and conversionistic. By denying any denominational identity, they try to appeal to the broadest possible Protestant audience and attract disaffected Catholics.

The remarkable growth of non-denominational groups shows that their strategy worked. *Christianity Today* computed that "using a baseline average from 1972–1976, over the last four decades, there has been more than a 400 percent growth in Protestants who identify as nondenominational."[218]

The *mega-church* movement takes the non-denominational model one step farther. These groups remove anything that would impede people from sitting in their pews—and then they remove the pews, too. If traditional church music turns you off, the organ and choir are replaced with a contemporary rock band. Don't like sermons? The preacher and sermons are replaced with theater and high-level entertainment. The messages vary. Many preach a utilitarian ethic, where happiness becomes the goal for the here and now, mixed with a call to make a "decision for Christ."

Although mega-churches are geared toward supplying the lowest common Christian-like beliefs for popular consumption, they do propound one unalterable, infallible dogma: all churches are the same. No church is more true or more beneficial than any other. This militant egalitarian approach to ecclesiology has a fatal flaw: if it doesn't matter where I go to church, why attend a mega-church? Why not satisfy my spiritual needs by myself and on my own terms? The mega-church cannot answer this question without forsaking its one infallible egalitarian dogma.

Unity, Mind Science, Therapeutic Christianity

Conversionism also truncates the Christian life. Outside certain streams of Protestant thought—such as the *Holiness Movement*—the goal of the Christian life after one "accepts Jesus" isn't very clear.

The *Mind Science* and *New Thought* movements attempt fill this gap by viewing Christianity as something therapeutic. Depending on the individual, Christian principles can be used to secure wealth, influence people, avoid suffering, attain physical healing, etc.

Several groups, already mentioned, have made forays into this area (e.g., Unity and Seventh-Day Adventists). One group we haven't mentioned is Christian Science. Founded by Mary Baker Eddy in 1875, Christian Science attempts

CHRISTIANITY BECOMES AN IDEA

to reform Christianity along therapeutic lines. In her book, *Science and Health with a Key to the Scripture*, Eddy proposes that illness is an illusion that can be cured through prayer. Not only is illness an illusion, but the whole world is also an illusion, and we can change the undesirable things in this illusion through our thoughts.

Christian Science and other Mind Science groups are not very influential. However, a book released in the 1950s popularizes the idea of therapeutic Christianity: *The Power of Positive Thinking* (1952) by Norman Vincent Peale. Peale posits that one can achieve a permanent and optimistic attitude, and a happier life, through habitual affirmations or visualizations. The author uses aspects of Christianity as a therapeutic tool for the betterment of the individual. What makes Peale's approach popular is that, unlike the Mind Science movement, its theology falls within the pale of mainline Protestant thought.

COMMUNITY
From Natural Law to Consequences Make Right

The truncation of the Christian life that leads to a therapeutic view of Christianity was preceded by an earlier truncation of the role of the clergy. When Luther abolishes the Mass and holy orders, Protestant clergy face an uneasy question:

> If clergy could neither absolve sin nor clear consciences, what was their appropriate function to be? Perhaps the best that could be offered was moral instruction—which

is to say, lessons in how to control oneself. The prevention of sin would have to replace its repentance. Since the provider of such instruction had no special authority or link with God, it followed that in moral matters he was obliged to give his proofs as well as his results.[219]

At first, Protestant clergy can apply scriptural principles in light of natural law, but when the Enlightenment rejects positive revelation and natural law, Scripture is no longer seen as a viable proof. If positive and natural law are no longer on the table, what else can anchor morality?

Locke appeals to experience. We desire happiness and recoil from pain. Moral feelings, therefore, can dictate to us what is good and what is evil. Locke's solution fits well with the Protestant commitment to direct communication between man and God. John Gay's essay, "Dissertation Concerning the Fundamental Principle of Virtue and Morality" (1731), connects the two.[220] Our happiness flows from virtuous action because God wishes us to be virtuous.

Although doing God's will can make us happy, as we noted at the beginning of the book, our transcendent desires show us that our ultimate happiness is found only in our beatific union with God.[221]

Without *religion*, secular society needs a goal to orientate itself. Therefore, people erase God from Gay's equation and hold that happiness is simply a product of human experience and psychological association. Natural happiness, thereby, becomes the goal, and society's mission is to maximize it.

Jeremy Bentham (1748–1832) and John Stuart Mill (1806–1873) believe they can maximize happiness through an ethic known as utilitarianism, in which right actions produce the greatest good for the greatest number of people.

But how can happiness be measured? Moreover, who decides what produces greater happiness than something else? What if fifty-one percent of the people think the greatest happiness can be achieved by executing the remaining forty-nine? There is a story, likely apocryphal, where one of Mill's students posed this question. Mill is said to have responded: "Englishmen would never do such a thing." The story, even if fictitious, is instructive.

Neither Mill nor Darwin can provide a rational response to the slaughter their systems could produce. The best they can do is appeal to a *noble instinct* that would prevent it. That *noble instinct* is nothing other than the Catholic cultural momentum. Back in Mill's day, it would have been unthinkable that the majority would slaughter the minority for the sake of greater happiness. But once society loses its momentum, the *noble instinct* begins to disappear, and totalistic states rear their ugly heads.

GOVERNMENT
The Advent of Totalistic States

Without God and his Church to cap its authority, the State becomes absolute, and the State's success becomes the greatest good. The beginning of the twentieth century brings forth a crop of totalitarian states who control and regulate virtually every aspect of their citizens' lives, or at least they try to. We are all familiar with Hitler's Germany (1933–1945), Mussolini's Italy (1925–1943), Stalin's Union of Soviet Socialist Republics (USSR) (1922–1991). The trend spreads east to Mao's People's Republic of China (1949–present), Kim's North Korea (1948–present), Pol Pot's Cambodia (1963–1997), and eventually Castro's Cuba (1958–present). Totalistic states may have existed in earlier times and in different cultures.[222] However, the eruption of these atheistic states at the beginning of the twentieth century in Christian countries suggests a common source: the tearing of the State from *religion*.

Without the Church, there is no moral capping authority to protect the citizens from the immoral actions of the State, and without God, the State becomes the highest law and the highest good. The citizens become for the State a means to an end. Those who become a hindrance or an inconvenience are eliminated. The death tolls of these atheistic totalistic states are staggering: the Soviet Union is responsible for around 61,911,000 deaths, China 35,236,000 deaths. Even the small country of Cambodia manages to kill 2,035,000 people, roughly a third of its population.[223]

HUMAN KNOWLEDGE
Science Reduced to a Tool

The golden age of the Dutch Republic was science and technology bent toward the acquisition of financial gains. Totalistic states bend science toward the advancement of national interests. In the 1970s, for example, the Soviet

Union's military and aerospace technology is cutting-edge, whereas its fields are being plowed by equipment that was outdated back in the 1930s. Embarrassed by this spectacle, the state quickly updates the machinery—not because it desires a well fed populace, but because updates further the state's goal to improve public opinion.

The *conflict myth* rails against dogmatic Christianity supposedly controlling and stifling scientific ideas. The secular atheistic states *actually do* control and stifle scientific ideas. Soviet scientists are not allowed to embrace Big Bang cosmology; it isn't compatible with the state's atheistic ideology because it implies creation. Instead, the more scientifically problematic *oscillating universe* theory is adopted because it seems to fit better with the dialectical materialism of Friedrich Engels, co-author of *The Communist Manifesto*. It isn't until the 1960s that the situation changes, and science in this area flourishes once again.[224]

Looking for Love in All the Wrong Places

Although natural happiness becomes the goal for secular life, its definition—without God—remains allusive. What is happiness? Is it the free acquisition of goods with no limits? Is it exterminating the minority to bring about the majority's greater happiness? Is it the ability to do what will make us most free—or what will eventually enslave us? Even if one option stands out, without God, there is no *religious ought* to insist that it must be so. Ultimately, whatever option we choose, it will fail to satisfy our transcendental desires for perfect truth, love, justice, beauty, and home. Without God, the quest to maximize happiness only maximizes dissatisfaction.

Although conversionism makes God intimately present during the conversion experience, it makes him distant in everything else. When combined with therapeutic Christianity and the search for satisfying natural happiness, we get what Christian Smith identified as *moralistic therapeutic deism*—the belief that God exists and makes no demands on us other than that we should *be nice*. Otherwise, he stands at attention, waiting to answer our prayers when we need help. Moralistic therapeutic deism quickly becomes the predominant belief among mainline and Evangelical Protestants as well as Catholic Americans in the early 2000s.

V.

SOCIAL REVOLT

Revolt Against Reality

At the heart of liberty is the right to define
one's own concept of existence, of meaning, of the
universe, and of the mystery of human life.

—JUSTICE ANTHONY KENNEDY

The Incarnation married faith and reason, theology and philosophy. It was this integration that sparked the many intellectual revolutions that brought about Western civilization. The Catholic genius was to combine knowledge and the Faith. This is why the Catholic Church was instrumental in the formation of what became the modern university.

After the Protestant Reformation, Protestants open their own religious schools. However, the ongoing religious conflicts and the Enlightenment call forth a new kind of secular education. In it, the unifying center of Christian education (theology and philosophy) is demoted to mere electives. The study of practical sciences takes their place—not as a unifying integrating principle, but as a group of fields of study among many. As Protestant divisions grow, more and more students join secular universities. The acceptance of the conflict myth, mentioned earlier, contributes to the popular view that religious or parochial schools are relics of the past. Secular institutions look down upon them as being backward, inferior, and medieval.

GOD AND CREATION
The Faith Becomes a Position

In the United States, Catholicism has always been a religious minority. Even though Catholics serve honorably in all the country's wars, anti-Catholic bigotry remains. Take for example the office of the president: there has always been a fear that if a Catholic is elected to the nation's highest office, he will become an agent of the pope and make Catholicism the established religion. These fears are fed by political and social propaganda from every angle, including the early nativist movement, the Know-Nothing Party (1845), and the Ku Klux Klan (1865).

Al Smith (1873–1944) becomes the first Catholic nominated by a major party to run for the presidency in 1928. Smith's popularity, bolstered with the newly minted women's vote, can't overcome the influence of the Klan. Conservative Southern white Democrats cross party lines and vote Republican out of fear that Smith will listen more to the pope than the Constitution. Smith loses.

In the 1960 election, Catholic John F. Kennedy (1917–1963) is nominated. Kennedy addresses the potential backlash to his Catholicism when he speaks to the Greater Houston Ministerial Association (September 12, 1960). He declares publicly that his Catholicism is a private matter.

> So it is apparently necessary for me to state once again not what kind of church I believe in—for that should be important only to me—but what kind of America I believe in. . . . For contrary to common newspaper usage, I am not the Catholic candidate for president. I am the Democratic Party's candidate for president, who happens also to be a Catholic. I do not speak for my Church on public matters, and the Church does not speak for me.
>
> Whatever issue may come before me as president—on birth control, divorce, censorship, gambling, or any other subject—I will make my decision in accordance with these views, in accordance with what my conscience tells me to be the national interest, and without regard to outside religious pressures or dictates. And no power or threat of punishment could cause me to decide otherwise.[225]

We've already seen how the *double truth* of the Latin Averroists turned the Catholic faith into *a position* and how Locke relegated *religion* to a purely private, interior, and spiritual matter distinct from the public, external, material workings of the secular order. So why do Kennedy's comments calm the anti-Catholic opposition? Effectively, Kennedy reduces Catholicism to a denomination. His explanation opens the possibility that some parts of divine law are not beneficial or good for society, thereby placing divine law and human law into two separate (possibly contradictory) spheres.

The Kennedy campaign signals a new direction for Catholics who wish to rid themselves of their Catholic inferiority complex. All they need to do is accept Locke's *private religion* idea. Consequently, we find today Catholic politicians who will sell themselves as Democrat or Republican candidates "who happen to be Catholic." They may attend daily Mass, march in St. Patrick's Day parades, and boast about their Catholic upbringing as they actively promote gravely immoral things—and even support legislation that undermines the safety and security of the Church—as a public good!

Catholic educators also see Kennedy's solution as a way to get out of the Catholic educational ghetto. Catholic educators in the late 1950s see their jobs as encumbered by their Catholicism. The rebellion begins on July 20, 1967, when Notre Dame president Fr. Theodore M. Hesburgh (1917–2015) gathers a small group of Catholic academic leaders in Land O' Lakes, Wisconsin to declare independence from Church authority. The millions of dollars raised by Catholics over the years to build these Catholic institutions are usurped and co-opted to form entirely different entities, seemingly overnight:

> Following the Land O' Lakes gathering, Catholic colleges removed most priests and nuns from their governing boards, and some secularized their mission statements.

Some Catholic colleges went so far as to remove crucifixes from classrooms and saintly statues from their grounds. Manhattanville College of the Sacred Heart and Webster College (now Webster University) publicly declared themselves "no longer Catholic." Manhattanville promptly deleted the "Catholic part" of its name; Webster College president Sister Jacqueline Grennan renounced her religious vows and withdrew from her religious order to become a lay leader so that she could lead the now-secular institution "without the embarrassment of being subject to religious obedience."[226]

Fr. Hesburgh will later write:

The best and only traditional authority in the university is intellectual competence. . . . A great Catholic university must begin by being a great university that is also Catholic.[227]

Sound familiar? It sounds a lot like Kennedy's self-description. According to this new view, a great university is essentially a secular university that offers daily Mass and a few electives in religion. The secularization effectively unmoors the Catholic university system from the comprehensive worldview that started it along with the religious imperative that brought about revolutions in science. Unlike in Europe, America's dismantling of Catholic education comes from within.

Among the greatest crimes committed by the Catholic education revolt is the hijacking of millions of dollars and man-hours Catholics had donated to build institutions for the formation and instruction of their children. After the revolt, Catholic parents have to struggle to pay hefty tuitions to send their children away to these same institutions, only to have those children graduate with a battered and bruised faith—if any faith at all. Faithful Catholics become impoverished while their unformed or ill formed children win high-paying jobs and gain positions of power.

Once again, we have the *double truth* idea—only this time, it infects Catholic universities, so that now we have Catholic universities allowing and even promoting anti-Catholic speakers to proselytize on their campuses, not to mention honoring public officials who champion legislation that directly violates the Church's core moral teachings.

The revolt in Catholic education reaches its peak with the coup at the Catholic University of America in 1967–68. The Catholic University of America is a pontifical university, under the direct control of the Holy See. The coup begins when the board of trustees decides not to renew the contract of a non-tenured professor, Fr. Charles Curran (b. 1934). Curran is a popular teacher who has become well known for his heterodox views on Catholic moral teachings. The bishops who inform Curran that they are not going to renew his contract provide no explanation for his termination, so Curran threatens to go to the press, claiming that the Church is violating the standards of academic freedom.

A media blitz and campus protests follow. Eventually, the bishops and trustees relent, renew Curran's contract, and even give him tenure.[228]

At the heart of the coup is the question of whether bishops are competent to judge whether theologians and academics can teach at the pontifical university. Curran and others argue that they aren't and rally public support to win the day. The fact that this revolution takes place in a pontifical university sends shockwaves throughout Catholic academia. If the bishops, who have direct oversight over what is being taught at a pontifical university, no longer have any real control, certainly, ordinary Catholic colleges and universities are exempt as well.

The coup creates, in effect, a shadow magisterium of "experts," which to varying degrees replace the bishops' ordinary magisterial role as instructors of the Faith. In the last chapter, we saw how Higher Criticism drove a wedge between mainline Protestant pastors and the unquestioned authority of "experts." Now, in the name of academic freedom, the "experts," not the Church, control what is being taught in Catholic universities.

The Second Vatican Council

The documents of the Second Vatican Council (1962–1965) are sober and easy to understand. However, a cadre of "experts," like those mentioned above, insinuate themselves into the position of being the official interpreters of the council. It is they who promote *the spirit of Vatican II*, which causes much destruction within the Church. Where the council calls for the laity to sanctify the temporal order, the experts promote the secularization of the sacred order. Unfortunately, many Catholics listen to them.

When Catholic academicians break with the visible Magisterium of the Church, they inadvertently turn the Faith into a kind of gnosis, accessible only to the knowing ones. It's not surprising that the *spirit of Vatican II* is anti-incarnational, bearing a strong resemblance to what we've seen in the Protestant revolt. Churches are stripped of their paintings, statues, and bells and smells. Realistic representations of Christ and his saints are replaced by unrealistic depictions and abstract art.

Perhaps most damaging of all is that the Eucharist—the extension of the Incarnation in human history, which once was the focal point for the congregation—is de-emphasized and its tabernacle sidelined. The desacralization of the Church combined with poor catechesis and evangelism undoubtedly contributes to Catholics losing their faith in Christ's real and substantial presence in the Eucharist. Without the Eucharist, there is no visible Church. Without the visible Church, the Faith becomes an idea—one idea among many.

Pre-Vatican II Problems

The seeds for these revolts within Catholicism were sown long before Vatican II. The Church emerging from the two great world wars is blessed with a flood of seminarians and a growing Catholic population. To accommodate the influx, religious instruction becomes streamlined, if not a bit distilled, ossified, and mechanical. Seminary instruction becomes manualistic.

By the 1950s, bishops become less like shepherds of the flock and more like the administrators of a large company. Catholic immigrants, struggling to rebuild their lives after the war, cede the religious education of their children to the parish priests, nuns, and religious. The result is clericalism, where the clergy become masters, not servants, of those in their care.

Clericalism takes on a concrete form in America when Cardinal John Dearden (1907–1988) retools the old system of prelates and pastors in the National Conference of Catholic Bishops (NCCB) and the United States Catholic Conference (USCC) into a new, efficient deliberative body modeled after the auto industry. With the aid of the Booz Allen Hamilton management consulting firm, Dearden re-engineers these bodies to function like the automotive Big Three. This may have seemed like a sensible idea back in 1966, when the Big Three ruled the auto manufacturing world, but as Detroiters painfully learn in the 1970s, it is precisely their grossly inefficient and bureaucratic management that leads to the demise of American dominance in the auto industry. Whether real or psychological, Dearden's overhaul doesn't help the Church break the bonds of clericalism.

Clericalism may contribute to the bishops' ineffectual response to dissenters in the 1960s. In fairness to those bishops, they are dealing with problems that they have never faced before. They know how to respond to attacks from outside the Church, but not attacks from their own flock, especially when the sheep show no scruples about joining ranks with anti-Catholics in the media.

Clericalism's worst effect is that it sets the stage for the most destructive blow to the Church's moral credibility in centuries: the sexual abuse scandal.

It's true that sexual predators exist in every walk of life, within every faith, and in every secular institution. But what makes the Church's sexual abuse scandal so destructive is the public statements prelates make to the press: bishops sound more like lawyers than shepherds. Rather than admitting their own personal failure and perhaps stepping down from their place in leadership, they blame the "experts" who had told them that predator priests could be reformed. Instead of confessing that they had placed the welfare of the clergy above the safety of their flock, they circle the wagons.

What makes this so unbecoming, even for non-Catholics, is the intuitive sense that the clergy is a visible sign of Christ's love for the Church. A husband is called to lay down his life for his bride in imitation of Christ, but these leaders, in a similar position, refuse to lay down their positions in reparation for their malfeasance. The press recognizes this. Smelling the blood in the water, secular media outlets go after the Church, often ignoring abuse stories in other areas. In this, they successfully brand Catholicism with the stamp of pedophilia, even though the vast majority of the clergy never did anything dishonorable.

Rebel Without a Cause

Vatican II causes a seismic shift within Protestantism. Almost overnight, Protestantism loses what was left of its Protestant identity. For centuries, the image of Luther defiantly standing alone, the righteous rebel, against the powers of the papacy and the emperor, was the paradigm for what it meant to be Protestant. Even those who disagreed with Luther's version of doctrinal purity affirmed his cause to be just. It was Catholicism (or rather, opposition to Catholicism) that unified and identified Protestantism. Whenever Catholicism affirmed something, Protestantism strengthened its resolve against it.

By the 1950s and 1960s, the disintegration of mainline Protestantism is nearing completion. It has become theologically liberal, with key Christian teachings either watered down or rejected entirely. As the mainline groups' membership age and dwindle, more conservative Protestant denominations grow.

Then Pope St. John XXIII (1881–1963) calls the Second Vatican Council. This council is different from the Church's previous ones in that it is pastoral. There are no anathemas or condemnations. It even invites Protestant and Orthodox observers. The overall tone is conciliatory, and *ecumenism* is the buzzword. The pope who closes the council, Pope St. Paul VI (1897–1978), is anything but an imperial pope. Indeed, one could argue that Paul VI's reticence to enforce discipline ultimately contributes to instability within the Church. Nevertheless, the single galvanizing force behind

Protestant identity has fallen. Its great foe has vanished from the battlefield, and the Protestant righteous rebel needs a new cause.

The upheaval over social issues in the 1960s becomes a new way for Protestants to carry on the virtuous rebellion, especially among the youth. This is nothing new. Mainline and liberal branches of Protestantism engaged in the *Social Gospel Movement* back in the last half of the nineteenth century. But as Protestant identity erodes, more begin describing themselves as "an anti-segregationist" and "for peace" rather than "a Baptist" or "a Presbyterian." With this, the battle shifts from doctrinal purity to social purity, and nominalist atomization, specialization, and polemics are transferred to the "secular world."

However, social change is a vehicle. It needs someone or something to drive it; it needs a solid religious and philosophical foundation. By this point in history, neither the waning Catholic cultural momentum nor fractured Protestant theology can take the wheel. What remains is interior religion and the dictates of unformed (or ill formed) conscience.

HUMAN INTEGRITY AND VALUE
The Identity-Struggle Fusion

Fighting for justice is indeed a great virtue, but when the struggle becomes our identity, the struggle becomes the primary, if not exclusive, source of our self-worth and self-esteem. What if the struggle ends? What will happen to our identity and self-worth? These too disappear.

The fusion of struggle and personal identity gives the warrior a strong incentive never to concede defeat or achieve victory. Both would make the righteous rebel obsolete, a warrior without a war to fight in. Therefore, the struggle must continue through an endless treadmill of causes to bring about social purity—that is, an unobtainable utopia.

Human dignity is rooted in what we are—made in the image and likeness of God—not what we do. Our actions can ennoble us, or they can degrade us, but our value remains. But under a nominalist worldview, which emphasizes the will over nature, *what we do* becomes the root of our dignity. If you're diminished in your capacity to act or think, you are less human.

It also cripples rational discourse: we are no longer individuals holding a position. Rather, we become the embodiment of that position, so even the most charitable critique from one's opponent is seen as a vitriolic personal attack.

The Women's Movement

The feminist movement, in its original form, campaigns primarily for women's suffrage and a ban on the sale of alcohol. In the early twentieth-century United States, *first-wave* feminists, as they will eventually be called, achieve these goals with the ratification of the Eighteenth Amendment (1919) and the Nineteenth Amendment (1920) to the U.S. Constitution. (The former, banning the sale of alcohol, will be repealed via the Twenty-First Amendment in 1933.)

After women won the right to vote in the 1920s, there was widespread belief that the political fight for women's liberation in the U.S. was over. Feminism virtually disappeared from the public stage as Americans struggled during the Great Depression to put food on the table and then rallied to fight World War II. But in the 1950s and '60s, prosperity returned, and comsumerism exploded. . . . America was swept up in the consumerist quest for possessions and status. That's when Betty Friedan appeared on the scene and launched the second-wave feminist movement.[229]

The *second wave* of feminism, whose members purport to campaign for equality among the sexes, initiate a drive for social purity that quickly divides their movement on an important issue: what does feminism really mean? Is it fiscal equality with men in the workplace? Is it the eradication of feminine stereotypes? Or is it the denial of the physical differences between the sexes?

Then, starting around the 1960s, *gender feminism* comes along . . . and blows these questions out of the water. For gender feminists, feminism is the recognition of and opposition to endemic and systemic oppression of women by the *patriarchy* (rule of men). With the ascendancy of gender feminism, the recognition of oppression becomes the *sine qua non* for being a feminist. Given its subjective and unquantifiable goals, gender feminism, like other movements that fuse struggle and identity, will be perpetually at war.

The Second Sex

The main avenue of action taken up by the 1960s gender feminists is trailblazed by Simone de Beauvoir in her book *The Second Sex* (1949). In it, de Beauvoir seeks to liberate women from servitude by separating them from womanhood. Put bluntly, women are free only to the extent that they become like men. Since female biology is so intimately tied to nature, de Beauvoir argues, female liberation must come by breaking (sometimes violently) those things that tie women to pregnancy and childrearing. This severing can be accomplished through abortion and state-run childcare.

De Beauvoir's reasoning sounds like the proposals of the Gnostics, who also recognized how female biology is intimately tied to nature, which they considered evil. Salvation is therefore possible only for women "who make themselves male."[230] For de Beauvoir, women need to become like men—not to enter the kingdom of heaven, but to be part of the kingdom of this world.

But can a woman *really* become like a man? Are the words *man* and *woman* really just labels, as the nominalists believe? De Beauvoir rejects this nominalist solution because "it is easy for antifeminists to show that women *are* not men."[231] This is 1949. Biological differences are obvious. But these differences become blurred with the introduction of the first birth control pill in 1960. The Pill virtually erases the connection between the marital act and procreation. The nominalist position begins to appear plausible.

The introduction of the Pill combines several earlier revolts into a perfect storm: acquisitiveness; the rejection of teleology; the de-integration of body and soul; utilitarianism; the eugenic elimination of the imperfect, weak, and unwanted; the objectification of women; and on and on.

The Battle of the Sexes

Later gender feminists take up the cause of making *man* and *woman* into mere social labels through extravagant social engineering projects. Frankly, some of their methods border on the bizarre; they include everything from no longer naming tropical storms and hurricanes exclusively with female names to sports spectaculars such as *The Battle of the Sexes*, the 1973 tennis match between Billie Jean King and Bobby Riggs, where the fifty-year-old Riggs loses to number-one-ranked King, then twenty-nine. These events are designed to promote the idea that men and women are essentially the same.

Sexual Reductionism

Here, two influential and opposite movements align. The Women's Movement seeks to make women equal to men by being sexually available without any biological consequences through artificial contraception and abortion. The Sexual Revolution, likewise, promotes unrestricted sexual availability. Feminist Helen Gurley Brown (1922–2012) promotes the notion that female sexual availability is a way to achieve personal empowerment. This worldview is promoted through a coordinated media campaign of women's magazines, often using "real-life stories" that are pure fabrications.[232]

The combination of these movements plus the explosion of pornography further reduces people's value to their sexual desirability, activity, and preferences.

Marriage Redefined

All religious traditions have seen homosexual acts as intrinsically disordered. Even in ancient pagan cultures, where these acts were tolerated, they were never given the same dignity as marriage. But with the abandonment of natural law and teleology, widespread artificial contraception that suppresses the link between sex and procreation, and militant egalitarianism, homosexuality becomes viewed as just a normal alternative to heterosexuality.

To sell this idea to the public, a *born this way* campaign begins. Since morality involves free will and free acts, an effort is made to prove that homosexuality is genetically predetermined in an unalterable way. Since something genetically predetermined cannot be reversed, homosexuality falls more in the realm of a civil right than a moral action. The search for the *gay gene* is on.

The propaganda campaign backfires, however, once activists realize that if a genetic link can be found, it can be used to predict whether a child will become homosexual (and perhaps to eugenically abort him). Or perhaps a cure can be found. Furthermore, studies appear that show that homosexuals can become long-term and stable heterosexuals, which speaks against biological predetermination. Unlike race, which is unalterable, sexual preferences can change.

The propaganda campaign succeeds in that it effectively moves the issue of same-sex attraction into the realm of race. There is already a large body of legislation on the books that penalizes discrimination against racial minorities. Once the public becomes convinced that sexual orientation belongs in the same category as race, the homosexual lobby is able to plug into this legislation and use the coercive power of the State against anyone who does not support its agenda.

Homosexual activism begins to put an end to anti-homosexual bullying and assaults. Activists then turn their focus to a string of unending social battles, which results in the same movement now becoming the worst kind of bully. Assaults, public harassment, and even financial and professional ruin can be unleashed against anyone who does not toe the party line.

No-Fault Divorice Becomes Widespread

The marriage contract continues to be enforced in America until 1969, when California becomes the first state to grant no-fault divorces. Under this law, either spouse can break the marital contract without any repercussions. But the whole purpose of a contract is to bind each party to hold up his end of the agreement. With no-fault divorce, marriage, the most solemn and sublime agreement a man and a woman can make, becomes *the exception* to this definitional rule of contracts.

Widespread no-fault divorce spurs a devaluation of marriage as a whole. As far as the State is concerned, marriage isn't even a real contract; it is more of a formality.

The spread of no-fault divorce contributes to a 250-percent increase in divorces from the 1960s to the 1980s, with seventy-five percent of applicants citing "lack of commitment."[233]

About half of all marriages today end in divorce. Forty percent of first marriages fail, compared with 16 percent in 1960, and 60 percent of remarriages fail. Three-fifths of all divorces involve minor children.[234]

Disposable marriage and widespread cohabitation have dire consequences for wives and children. Initially, the most disastrous result of no-fault divorces, outside making a spouse disposable, is that it favors the spouse who is best suited to survive alone economically. This usually means that husbands fare better than their wives after a divorce. Since the court usually favors the mother over the father in terms of custody of the children, divorced women with children are at a decided economic disadvantage. This is one of the reasons behind the "feminization of poverty" that takes place between the 1970s to the 1990s in the United States.

In the 1980s, the divorce rate begins to level off and then to drop. Why the drop? As author Daniel Davis notes:

Generation X was the first of the collateral damage. Roughly half of all children born to married parents in the 1970s saw their parents' divorce, a massive increase from just 11% of kids born in the 1950s.[235]

These children are deeply scarred by the experience of disposable marriages. Millennials choose not to marry; they just cohabit. Divorces drop because the number of marriages drop. Not only is marriage avoided, but it becomes socially acceptable to have children out of wedlock, even on purpose.

THE CHURCH
Nons and Nones

With the explosion of the *new atheism*, a new statistic also appears: the *non-affiliated*. Many understand this category to consist mainly of atheists and agnostics. That is partly true. It is really the natural fallout from the *non-denominational* and *mega-church* movements, which created yet another denomination: the *spiritual, but not religious*. This is a retreat to the religious instinct of deism, where people can attempt to fulfill their inner desire of what they believe God to be in the most individualistic way possible—a kind of do-it-yourself project. The non-affiliated denomination inherits its predecessors' militant egalitarianism. This too is a revolt against reality.

Militant egalitarianism denies that any one religion or thought system truly sees reality as it is; all are equal in that they are all equally wrong. Once this view is adopted as a social dogma, it produces a myriad of cases of institutionalized indifference, such as the Satanic Temple of Southern Florida being allowed to open Pensacola's city council session with a satanic prayer.[236] Similar petitions have been made by other groups around the country. The social dogma dictates that all religions and belief systems are equal, but is Satanism really equal to Christianity? As long as blind militant egalitarianism continues, more and worse absurdities will undoubtedly arise.

Some views grasp reality more fully or clearly than others. To that extent, they promote human flourishing and the common good. Militant egalitarianism denies any intrinsic differences among cultures and beliefs, so the State ends up, in many cases, protecting what harms it.

GOVERNMENT
The Atomization of Liberty

The irrational fruit of nominalism can be seen in the U.S. Supreme Court decisions in the last few decades. Unhinged from natural law, the Supreme Court has begun to mirror the nominalist god, who arbitrarily rules something right or wrong. There is no better example of the disconnect between the High Court and reality than Justice Anthony Kennedy's "mystery of life" opinion in *Planned Parenthood v. Casey*:

At the heart of liberty is the right to define one's own concept of existence, of meaning, of the universe, and of the mystery of human life.[237]

In this case, it is at the heart of liberty for a woman to kill her innocent and helpless unborn baby so long as her own "concept of existence" includes the idea that her baby is not a baby. One wonders what would happen if American citizens adopted a "concept of existence" that doesn't include the Supreme Court. Would they be at liberty to dismiss its ruling?

Under the equal protection clause of the United States Constitution, the Supreme Court rules that people of the same sex can be married. Although marriage is hailed as a right, which means that it is accessible to all, such was never the case. Not everyone could marry. There were always sanguinity laws that prevented near blood relations from marrying. There were other restrictions as well. These restrictions were ordered for the good of the potential offspring. But with marriage disconnected from nature and offspring, what prevents two brothers or two sisters from getting married to each other? What about a child marrying his parent? Or why restrict marriage to humans only? Can a human marry an animal? Can a human marry an inanimate object?

Indeed, the redefinition of marriage makes it so broad that it must eventually encompass such bizarre cases. Much like John Stuart Mill's alleged reply to his student, people couldn't imagine that their fellow citizens would propose such things, yet they have.

Gender Confusion

Since activists who fuse their identity with their struggle must always be at war against an opponent, almost immediately after its victory in the Supreme Court with regard to marriage, the gay rights movement transforms into the *LGBT movement*, which turns into the *LGBTQ movement*, which then turns into *LGBTQIA* only to become *LGBTQIA+*. Like all nominalist endeavors, the subject becomes atomized until it reaches the level of isolated individuals. The plus sign is placed at the end of *LGBTQIA* so that each individual not covered by a letter will be included. To resurrect Martin Luther's comment, there are almost as many genders and sexual identifications as there are heads.

Sexuality has become a social convention. If a man sees himself as a female—wears female clothing and makeup, does girly things—he can identify himself as a woman. A female who cuts her hair "like a boy" and does "boy things" can identify herself as a boy. What *gender identity* does is institutionalize the same sexual stereotypes that the gender feminist movement sought to stamp out. Indeed, the feminist movement has itself become a social convention—a "girly thing" that girls do—leading us to the bizarre spectacle of men who identify themselves as women by engaging in female sexual stereotypes joining women's marches to oppose the oppressive patriarchy's encouragement of sexual stereotypes. You might have to take a moment and chart out the logic on paper. It's almost too insane to follow without a visual aid.

Nominalism is at the heart of the gender movement. It denies that God created living things "according to their kind" and proposes that we can determine our own nature. It also suggests divine deception in that God made you appear male even though you are actually female.

There is also an iconoclastic element to this movement. Our bodies are icons of our souls, in that the dispositions of the soul are manifested through the body. The gender movement destroys this connection and turns the will of the soul against the body, even to the point of violently imposing a new identity by effacing the body and recreating it into something other than what it is. Vatican II's words, "when God is forgotten . . . the creature itself grows unintelligible," seem prophetic in retrospect.[238]

The Separation of the State from Religion

Militant egalitarianism also leads to the suppression of any religious language or references to God, even in the United States' founding documents! It is becoming more and more frequent to hear politicians quoting the "self-evident" "unalienable rights" of "life, liberty, and the pursuit of happiness" from the Declaration of Independence while deliberately skipping over that these rights exist because people "are endowed by their Creator" with them. Even the deistic "God of nature" has now become too offensively sectarian for public speech.

The idea of *freedom of religion* is also redefined to *freedom of worship*. You are free to believe and worship however you like as long as you do so within your church or temple. Whereas non-Catholic religions may comfortably live with such a compromise, such is not the case with Catholicism. The Mass is where St. Paul commands us to "present your bodies as a living sacrifice" (Rom. 12:1) in union with Christ, our head, to God the Father in the Holy Spirit. This means that our everyday lives are intimately connected with the Mass. Freedom of worship, for Catholics, means the freedom to live out our Christian vocation in everything we do.

Earlier, we saw how *freedom of worship* was used to suppress Catholics speaking out against injustices, as when Hitler railed against critical clergy as "politicizing priests."

Irreligion Hijacks No-Popery History

On September 11, 2001, Islamic terrorists attack the United States. A small cadre of outspoken atheists use this crisis as an opportunity to promote the idea that all religion is inherently violent and that unless it is suppressed, it will kill us all. These *new atheists* hijack the old no-popery history, Whig history, and conflict myths of the past, changing them from their original intent (anti-Catholicism; anti-dogmatic Christianity) to anti-theism. It is no longer just Catholicism, but all religions that promote ignorance, superstition, and violence. Now secular atheism is the promoter of enlightenment, progress, and peace.

Although the *new atheistic* enterprise uses no-popery myths to poison, disparage, and insult its opponents, it does so without proposing any substantive arguments. It proposes instead that all religion is ridiculous because it can be ridiculed. Ridiculing a position, however, is not the same as refuting it. Unfortunately, the collapse of religious instruction and catechesis had cleared the way for the remarkable success of this kind of propaganda, and, seemingly overnight, atheism and irreligion take a leap forward in credibility.

Bias Confirmation, Fake News, and Conspircy Theories

When ridicule is substituted for refutation, a belief no longer stands on evidence. Rather, it constantly needs to be reinforced by emotionally reaffirming content. This niche had already begun to be filled by the invention of *infotainment* in the 1980s, when "news" programs were designed to promote a one-sided viewpoint. The proliferation of these curated bias-confirming outlets created a market that looks similar to the ideal environment for Protestant church-shoppers, who seek out places of worship that agree with what *they* think Jesus taught. Now individuals pick what version of the news fits what they believe.

Social media, driven by bias-confirming content, further atomizes communities into factions, isolated by their own curated information silos or echo chambers. Discussions are reduced to slogans, cliches, name-calling, labels, and the promotion of an *us versus them* tribal mentality.

The desire for bias confirmation makes people more susceptible to *fake news* and *disinformation*: baseless stories designed to make the implausible appear plausible. It works along the same line as the propaganda technique of Hitler's *big lie*:

> The broad masses of a nation are always more easily corrupted in the deeper strata of their emotional nature than

consciously or voluntarily; and thus in the primitive sim-
plicity of their minds they more readily fall victims to
the big lie than the small lie, since they themselves often
tell small lies in little matters but would be ashamed to
resort to large-scale falsehoods. It would never come into
their heads to fabricate colossal untruths, and they would
not believe that others could have the impudence to distort the truth so infamously. Even though the facts which
prove this to be so may be brought clearly to their minds,
they will still doubt and waver and will continue to think
that there may be some other explanation. For the grossly
impudent lie always leaves traces behind it, even after it
has been nailed down.[239]

Fake news offers an alternative explanation for the world
around us. Even after it is debunked, it still "leaves traces
behind it"—*perhaps there may be an element of truth there!*

We encountered *fake news* throughout history, beginning
with the serpent's lie in Genesis 3:

In the account of the first sin, the tempter approaches
the woman by pretending to be her friend, concerned
only for her welfare, and begins by saying something only
partly true. . . . After listening to the deceiver and letting
herself be taken in by his version of fact, the woman was
misled. . . . The tempter's "deconstruction" then takes on
an appearance of truth.[240]

The result is a proliferation of conspiracy theories, inside knowledge, and unverifiable assertions, claiming to enlighten us as to what *really* is going on. Unfortunately, this phenomenon is found in Catholic outlets along with secular ones.

It Is Not Good for Man to Be Alone

Radical individualism has reached a point where community is replaced by tribalism and each person lives within his own virtual bubble universe. During World War II, people flock to the movie theaters to escape the brutal reality of the war. During the 1950s, televisions become popular, and families can escape the crowds by staying at home to watch whatever they choose for free over public airwaves. Cable and satellites carve out their own niche market, providing first run movies, sporting events, and pornography for those willing to pay for it. Livestreaming makes it possible for people to escape their families and retreat into their own worlds via cell phones and other devices. All this for the price of the device, an internet provider, and intrusive commercials. Texting and social media replace unmediated face-to-face discussions. Individuals have become imprisoned within a virtual world, surrounded by a wall of social media. Unlike the Incarnation, the constant and ever-growing bombardment of communication hasn't united humanity; it has instead caused an epidemic of loneliness.

Me, My Pet, and I

Multi-generational homes, which were once the norm, become single-family homes. With the collapse of marriage, "over a quarter of the U.S. population—and 28 percent of older adults—now live by themselves," according to the U.S. Census Bureau.[241] A growing percentage of people don't know anyone who truly knows them well. Despite all the connectivity, they feel isolated.

According to a recent poll, "forty-one percent of Britons say the TV or a pet is their main source of company, and the U.K. has created a cabinet level minister to deal with the problem of rampant loneliness."[242] Stephanie Coontz, a historian at Evergreen State College, spells it out with special clarity: "As we gain the freedom to become whatever we want to be, we've lost the sense of belonging."[243]

In the end, we have become alienated from God who became flesh, alienated from each other, and even alienated from our own bodies. Man is once again alone with the animals (Gen. 2:18–19).

Reality Strikes Back

The light shines in the darkness,

and the darkness has not overcome it.

—JOHN 1:5

History has a way of grinding bad ideas down to their illogical conclusions. The end result is insanity. This seems to be where we are headed now. It would take more than a book to describe the strange incoherence we live in.

Consider this: businesses need customers to survive. However, today, we have corporations contributing millions of dollars to Planned Parenthood, which promotes the suppression and execution of future customers! On the other hand, we have parents pushing their pre-teens to "sex change" operations because they "feel" trapped in the opposite sex's body. Then we have the even more bizarre cases, such as a mother who wishes to marry her son and daughter.[244] A well known personality's appearance on a popular podcast was canceled because she had dared to tweet that "only women can give birth."[245] The list goes on.

But no matter how much we try to ignore or reconceptualize it, reality always has the last word. Even now, in this present darkness and chaos, it is possible to see reality breaking through the insanity.

Intellectual Conversions

One hopeful sign is the ongoing phenomenon of *intellectual conversions*. The most shocking of these is the conversion of Antony Flew (1923–2010), one of the foremost advocates of atheism in the twentieth century. Flew does not become Christian before his death, but the evidence compels him to change his mind that God does indeed exist.[246] There is also a steady stream of intellectual conversions to Catholicism by Protestant ministers, clergy, and lay leaders. The *Coming Home Network International*, an apostolate established to help clergy and laymen convert to Catholicism, reports in January 2020 that it has helped 1,319 Protestant clergy members come into communion with the Church.

Catholic Education

Catholic education also turns a corner, due in large part to the efforts of Pope St. John Paul II (1920–2005). During the 1960s coup, the battle is couched as the academics on one side and the miters on the other side. The pontificate of John Paul II changes the battlefield. On August 15, 1990, the pope, a world-class philosopher and theologian by anyone's standards, issues the apostolic constitution *Ex Corde Ecclesiae* (On Catholic Universities), where he sets forth the mission and norms that Catholic universities ought to follow. The major Catholic universities contemptuously ignore *Ex Corde*, but others embrace it. Catholic parents find that they suddenly have a new option available to provide their children with a solid Catholic education. With newfound support, these smaller institutions grow rapidly. Although they may never reach the same size as the older universities—universities that "happen to be Catholic"—dioceses throughout the United States come to benefit from their positive influence.

Catholic middle-school and high-school education also undergoes a renaissance through the internet. Catholics and other religious-minded parents now have a viable alternative to secular education. As fewer men and women marry and have children, the economic pressures of operating brick-and-mortar schools will continue to tilt the scale toward home-based education. Solid Catholic groups will undoubtedly reap the benefits.

Although it remains to be seen, growing small Catholic higher education and homeschooling institutions may provide an answer to the mainline, mainstream religious education that has contributed to the clericalism problem. If so, clericalism may be on its way out.

Philosophy

In the 1960s and 1970s, atheist instructors—or at least decidedly anti-Christian instructors—dominate philosophy departments. Today, secular institutions face a resurgence of theist philosophers and philosophy.[247]

This renewal includes a resurgence of interest in the classical theism of the ancient Greeks; Muslims; and Christian thinkers, such as St. Thomas Aquinas. Where lowbrow atheism has grown on the popular level, theistic philosophy on the academic level is crackling with new life and vigor.

One promising offshoot within philosophy is called the *New Essentialism*, which provides a realistic approach to science that takes seriously *goal-directedness* or teleology as a real feature in nature. The New Essentialism may prove to be the key to reconnecting science with classical philosophy.

Bible and History

A series of quiet revolutions has also taken place in biblical and historical research. Where once Protestant biblical scholars undermined the importance of Sacred Tradition and the witness of the early Church, scholars now appeal to those very same early witnesses to vindicate the truth of Christ's life, death, and resurrection. This is a dangerous area to tread for a Protestant, since it raises the question: why restrict the early witness of the Church to only those points? Couldn't the Church Fathers and other early witnesses also supply reliable information about other things Jesus and the apostles taught, like the Real Presence or regenerative baptism?

Catholic biblical scholarship has undergone its own renaissance. Catholic biblical studies in the 1960s and 1970s on the academic level and parish level were dry and pedantic. The influx of scholarly converts has revitalized biblical scholarship in the Church. Suddenly, studying Scripture in light of Sacred Tradition is no longer considered *pre-Vatican II*. The renewal includes a newly discovered interest in the early Church Fathers and also the Jewish biblical roots of the Catholic faith. On a popular level, new high-quality biblical studies are being produced, and there is a newfound interest in the *lectio divina*, an ancient approach to studying, meditating on, and contemplating Scripture. These new approaches have made the older modernistic approaches appear lifeless and dated.

Secular historical research is also undergoing a silent revolution. Although the old no-popery myths about the Crusades, the Inquisition, and so on still circulate in high school and college textbooks, new cutting-edge secular historiography is the latest to expose and debunk these myths. It remains to be seen whether newer textbooks begin to reflect these new studies or not. However, there is hope. As the students of these historians become instructors, there may be a trickle-down effect from academia to the popular level. If this happens, Whig history may begin to disappear.

Gender Strikes Back

Even though the gender identity movement is still in its infancy, reality is already striking back in some interesting ways. One area is the issue of privacy and safety in women's restrooms. As soon as national chain department stores begin allowing males who call themselves women to use women's restrooms, there is an immediate outcry. People come face to face with the idea of having a male alone in a room with a partially dressed woman or young girl, and protests erupt. Some policies were changed. This is perhaps the only area to date where public pushback has had some effect.

Another area where reality may make a comeback is the one area that benefited the most from the feminist movement: women's sports. The battle of the sexes takes a nightmarish turn when men begin to compete "as women" in women sports, breaking a lot of women's records. If the trend continues, the public will need to affirm that there is an essential difference between men and women, no matter what they call themselves—or else women will no longer be able to fairly compete in women's sports.

Islam

There is some fear in Europe that Muslims will become a majority and install sharia law. This may be a legitimate fear, but Islam is facing its own crisis.

Islam's adoption of a radical kind of nominalism has crippled the intellectual and technical development of Islamic countries. As author Robert Reilly explains:

> The closure of the Muslim mind . . . is the key to unlocking such puzzles as why the Arab world stands near the bottom of every measure of human development; why scientific inquiry is nearly moribund in the Islamic world: why Spain translates more books in a single year than the entire Arab world has in the past thousand years: why

some people in Saudi Arabia still refuse to believe man has been to the moon; and why some Muslim media present natural disasters like Hurricane Katrina as God's direct retribution.[248]

Saudi Arabia, the heart of the Islamic world, imports large numbers of foreign laborers to build and maintain its modern infrastructure. In 2013, an estimated 8.55 million foreign workers (mostly non-Muslim) live and work in Saudi Arabia. Due to looming unemployment, the Saudi government makes an effort to thin out the ranks of foreigners living within its country, resulting in a twenty-two-percent drop in foreign workers over the past two years. The loss doesn't help Saudi unemployment.

Non-Muslim worship is forbidden in Saudi Arabia. Indeed, even non-Wahhabi Muslims generally do not receive permits to build their mosques. But on December 1, 2018, Egyptian and other Arab media report that, for the first time, a Coptic Mass has been held in Saudi Arabia, in the capital city of Riyadh. And as of late 2018 and early 2019, there are rumors that Saudi Arabia will allow the building of a Christian church to accommodate its foreign workers.

Demographic Winter

Reality also appears to be striking back in the area of population. We should note that demography is a speculative and changing field, so we need to speak tentatively. It appears that Paul Ehrlich's *Population Bomb* may turn out to be an implosion instead. The culture of death has managed to tip population growth below replacement levels in several countries. Widespread contraception, abortion, and people opting for the pleasures of modernity over parenthood have suppressed birth rates. At the same time, advances have enabled people to live longer, healthier lives, resulting in a world population that is quickly growing old.

So far, Europe and the Americas have avoided the economic effects of this demographic change, largely due to immigration. However, immigration alone will not lead to stability, since immigrant families quickly adopt the anti-life mentality of their host countries. Muslim families, for example, tend to have more children than their Christian counterparts. However, the high Muslim birth rate evaporates once they become implanted in the toxic atmosphere of modernity. Indeed, Western modernity has been exported into Muslim lands, with the result that they too are slowly growing older.

Spiritual but Not Fulfilled

Here is one hopeful sign concerns the "spiritual, not religious" category mentioned earlier. Despite their rejection of "organized religion," they have nevertheless rediscovered the wisdom of Catholic piety and spirituality. For a number of years, there has been an unexpected upsurge in pilgrimages and visits to shrines. Walking the Camino de Santiago de Compostela, known popularly as *the Way of St. James* or *the Camino*, has become a trend. According to the Society of St. James, 301,036 pilgrims received a certificate of completion in 2017, which is a sixty-seven-percent increase of pilgrims from 2004.[249] Catholic shrines have also seen an increase in visits, especially those tied to Marian apparitions such as the shrine in Knock, Ireland. This may be a sign that the old Whig history concerning the "Dark Ages" may be crumbling, and people may be starting to rediscover that medieval piety isn't fruitless or superstitious after all.

What accounts for all the push groups, political divisiveness, alienation, skepticism, and ugliness we find today? Perhaps it is reality reasserting itself.

In the beginning, God created us for himself, and so we all possess transcendental desires—the desire for perfect truth, love, goodness, justice, beauty, being, home. These desires can be suppressed, but they can never be extinguished. True happiness cannot be found in this world. It can only ultimately and most perfectly be found through the divine Son, who united heaven and earth in the Incarnation. Only through him can we be truly and fully united to God and to each other.

About the Author

Gary Michuta has been a popular speaker on Catholic apologetics and evangelization for more than twenty years. Through parish talks, seminars, and online classes he has helped hundreds of Catholics better understand and explain their Faith.

Gary is the former editor of *Hands On Apologetics Magazine* and has written seven books, including *How to Wolf-Proof Your Kids*, *Why Catholic Bibles Are Bigger*, *Making Sense of Mary*, *The Case for the Deuterocanon*, and *Hostile Witnesses: How the Enemies of the Church Prove Christianity*. He also writes the award-winning column "Behind the Bible" for the *Michigan Catholic* newspaper and is the host of "Hands On Apologetics" on Virgin Most Powerful Radio.

Gary and his wife, Christine, live in southeast Michigan with their three children, and he teaches middle- and high-school-level apologetics courses online for *Homeschool Connections*.

Endnotes

1   Kirsten Weir, "Worrying Trends in U.S. Suicide Rates," *Monitor on Psychology*, 50, no. 3 (March 2019), 24, apa.org/monitor/2019/03/trends-suicide.

2   The first creation (creation from nothing or *ex nihilo*) is taught in 2 Maccabees 7:28: "Recognize that God did not make them out of things that existed (οὐκ ἐξ ὄντων, *ex nihilo*)." Also Wisdom 1:14, Romans 4:17. The second creation is taught in Wisdom 11:17: "For thy all-powerful hand, which created the world out of formless matter" (cf. Genesis 1:2, MT) and Hebrews 11:3: "By faith we understand that the world was created by the word of God, so that what is seen was made out of things which do not appear" (cf. Genesis 1:2, LXX).

3   There are several words that overlap in meaning, such as *breath* and *life* (Hebrew, *ru'ach*; Greek, *pneu'ma*) and *soul* (Greek, *psychē*). Depending on the context, they can mean life (or the principle of life), the extension of the person, or the seat of rationality. Since the soul is the form of the body in that it animates the body and makes the body what it is, Scripture will often express this unity in odd ways, such as when Adam is described as a "living soul" (Gen. 2:7, KJV) or a "dead body" (Lev. 21:11; Num. 6:6).

4   Augustine, *Confessions,* 1,1-2.

5   St. Thomas Aquinas, *Summa Contra Gentiles* 3.70: "Accordingly just as it is not unreasonable that one action be produced by an agent and by the virtue of that agent, so is it not absurd that the same effect be produced by the inferior agent and by God, and by both immediately, though in a different way."

6   Gary Michuta, *Making Sense of Mary* (Nikaria Press, 2013).

7   This is a point seen by several early Church Fathers (see Irenaeus of Lyons, *Fragment 14*).

8   For example, Lamech in Genesis 4:23-24.

9   Roy Varghese, in *The Christ Connection: How the World Religions Prepared the Way for the Phenomenon of Jesus* (Paraclete Press: 2011), looks at these questions and finds lots of data in other religious thought and sacred texts that would open the door to embracing the gospel.

10 Ibid.

11   Ibid.

12   See David Twetten, "Aquinas and the Prime Mover of Aristotle.
      A Study of the Medieval Demonstration of God's Existence from
      Motion," (PhD diss., University of Toronto Centre for Medieval
      Studies, 1993), https://philpapers.org/rec/TWEAAT-2.

13   In 1 Samuel 7:7-10, God speaks to Samuel from the Ark, which is
      likewise associated with the cloud (see also 1 Kings 8:10-12).

14   This is a reference to the *second creation* (*createo secunda*) that we
      mentioned earlier in Genesis 1.

15   "All-powerful" (Greek, *pantodynamon*) and "overseeing all" (Greek,
      panepiskopon).

16   He does this out of the nature of his goodness. As Aquinas explains:
      "The very nature of God is goodness. . . . But it belongs to the essence
      of goodness to communicate itself to others. . . . Hence it belongs to
      the essence of the highest good to communicate itself in the highest
      manner to the creature, and this is brought about chiefly by 'his so
      joining created nature to himself that one Person is made up of these
      three—the Word, a soul and flesh,' as Augustine says (*De Trinitate* 13)"
      (*Summa Theologica*, III, q. 2, art. 1).

17   Stacy Trasancos, *Science Was Born of Christianity: The Teaching of Fr.
      Stanley Jaki* (Titusville, FL: The Habitation of Chimham Publishing
      Company, 2014), loc. 2254, Kindle.

18   Preserved in Origen's *Against Celsus*, 5:14. Emphasis mine.

19   Id., 49.

20   N.T. Wright, *Christian Origins and the Question of God,* vol. 3,
      The Resurrection of the Son of God (London: Society for Promoting
      Christian Knowledge, 2003), 35.

21   Michael Aquilina and James Papandrea, *Seven Revolutions: How
      Christianity Changed the World and Can Change It Again* (New York:
      Image Books, 2015), 106.

22   Ibid.

23   Peter Brown, *The Haskell Lectures on History of Religions*, ed. Joseph M.
      Kitagawa, vol. 2, *The Cult of the Saints: Its Rise and Function in Latin
      Christianity* (Chicago: University of Chicago Press, 1982), 10-11.

24   The Journey Home, "Dr. David Anders," February 8, 2010, on
      EWTN, https://www.youtube.com/watch?v=R5NT32Y-Mrk.

25   St. Jerome, *Letter 22*, 38.

26   Stacy Trasancos, "The Stillbirth of Science in Greece" Strange
      Notions, 2014, https://strangenotions.com/the-stillbirth-of-science-
      in-greece/.

27   "The pagan view of an external, inevitable force coercing and

controlling all action, whether human or divine, found itself in conflict with the conception of a free, personal, infinite God. Consequently, several of the early Christian writers were concerned to oppose and refute the theory of fate. But, on the other hand, the doctrine of a personal God possessing an infallible foreknowledge of the future and an omnipotence regulating all events of the universe intensified some phases of the difficulty. A main feature, moreover, of the new religion was the importance of the principle of man's moral freedom and responsibility. Morality is no longer presented to us merely as a desirable good to be sought. It comes to us in an imperative form as a code of laws proceeding from the sovereign of the universe and exacting obedience under the most serious sanctions" Michael Maher, "Fatalism," in *The Catholic Encyclopedia*, eds. Charles Herbermann, Edward Pace, Condé Pallen, Thomas Shahan, and John Wynne, vol. 5 (New York: Robert Appleton Company, 1909) https://www.newadvent.org/cathen/05791a.htm. newadvent.org/cathen/05791a.htm.

28 "In those in whose person he suffered when he said: 'Saul, Saul, why dost thou persecute me?' Therefore, let us serve Christ. He is with us in his followers; he is with us in ourselves: not without reason did he say: 'Behold, I am with you . . . even unto the consummation of the world" (Augustine, *Sermon 239*, 6). See also Basil the Great, *Letter VIII*, 8.

29 Unlike in English, the Greek uses two different words to signify whether the pronoun *you* is singular or plural.

30 Augustine, *Sermons on Selected Lessons of the New Testament*, Sermon 94 (144), 5 (4).

31 The foot of the Messiah alone that crushes the head of the serpent (Gen. 3:15, Ps. 109 [110]:1), yet Paul states that the serpent's head is crushed under the feet of Christians (Rom. 16:20), since "[the Father] put all things in subjection under his [Christ's] feet, and gave him as head over all things to the Church, which is his body, the fullness of the one who fills all things in every way" (Eph. 1:22-23, NAB).

32 Augustine, *City of God*, XVII, 18).

33 The Journey Home,"Dr. David Anders."

34 Aquilina and Papandrea, *Seven Revolutions*, 69.

35 With regard to the revolution as it relates to children, I recommend O.M. Bakke's *When Children Became People: The Birth of Childhood in Early Christianity* (Philadelphia: Fortress Press, 2005).

36 Augustine, *Exposition of the Psalms* (33-50), vol. 2, trans. M. Boulding, O.S.B. (Hyde Park, NY: New City, 2000), 133.

37   Michael Aquilina and James Papandrea, *How Christianity Saved Civilization and Must Do So Again* (Nashua, NH: Sophia Institute Press, 2019), 7-8.

38   The dilemma is found in Plato's dialogue *Euthyphro*, where Socrates asks Euthyphro, "Is the pious loved by the gods because it is pious, or is it pious because it is loved by the gods?" (10a). The divine command theory posits that God's command makes it good. One can see the same idea at work in society in that something becomes morally right or wrong by the State ruling it so.

39   Pliny the Younger, *Letter 10*:96.

40   *Gospel According to Thomas*, logion 114. It's possible that this last logion was a later addition because it seems in conflict with logion 22. However, the opposite is just as likely: "Due to the character of the *Gospel of Thomas* as a collection, the occurrence of different traditions is not surprising; it is a phenomenon also observed elsewhere in the *Gospel of Thomas*. It should be taken into consideration that in *Gos. Thom.* 22 the point of departure is the (genderless) child, but in *Gos. Thom.* 114, it is the (gender-defined) woman." Plisch, Uwe-Karsten, and Gesine Schenke Robinson, *The Gospel of Thomas: Original Text with Commentary* (Stuttgart: Deutscche Bibelhesellshaft Stuttgart, 2008).

41   Irenaeus of Lyons, *Against Heresies*, 3, 3, 1-3.

42   William Barry, "Arianism," in *The Catholic Encyclopedia*, eds. Charles Herbermann, Edward Pace, Condé Pallen, Thomas Shahan, and John Wynne, vol. 1 (New York: Robert Appleton Company, 1907), https://www.newadvent.org/cathen/01707c.htm.

43   Hilaire Belloc, *The Great Heresies* (Gastonia, NC: TAN Books, 2018), 22.

44   Vincent of Lérins, *Commonitory*; 2, 5-6.

45   See Rod Bennett's, *The Apostasy That Wasn't*, (El Cajon, CA: Catholic Answers Press, 2015).

46   "In fact, it seems characteristic of the Christian emperors of the fourth century down to Valentinian and Valens that they were almost all less than wholeheartedly devoted to the harsh pagan-Christian dichotomy which the ecclesiastical authorities tried to propagate. In religion, their tastes tended toward Arianism and semi-Arianism (a heresy notoriously adaptable to classicizing philosophical notions, open to the interpretation that the less-than-fully-divine Jesus was merely a mediator between the human and the divine, like any of the pagan deities), and their policy toward paganism tended toward lenience (tempered only by a revulsion from magical arts and nocturnal sacrifices—no doubt because those practices were so often employed in efforts to shorten the life expectancies of reigning emperors)."

James J. O'Donnell, *The Demise of Paganism, Traditio* 35 (1979), 45–88.

47 Jerome, *Against the Luciferians*, 19.

48 Quoted in Edward J. Chinnock, *A Few Notes on Julian and a Translation of His Public Letters* (London: David Nutt, 1901), 75–76.

49 See *Letter 36,* in *Julian, Volume III,* trans. Wilmer C. Wright, in Loeb Classical Library, vol. 157 (Cambridge, MA: Harvard University Press, 1923), 118.

50 Michael Aquilina, *The Healing Imperative: The Early Church and the Invention of Medicine as We Know It* (Steubenville, OH: Emmaus Road Publishing, 2018), loc. 1588–1595, Kindle.

51 Id., loc. 1736.

52 Hippolytus, *Refutation of All Heresies*, 9, 8. According to the description, the angel was of gigantic proportions and he was identified as the Son of God. The accompanying woman was identified as the Holy Spirit.

53 I.e., the Elchasaites and the Sabians. See Brian Bradford's *Muhammad's Jesus* (Scotts Valley, CA: CreateSpace Independent Publishing, 2015) for an excellent treatment on this subject.

54 All quotations from Muhammad M. Pickthall, ed., *The Quran* (Medford, MA: Perseus Digital Library, n.d.); Brian Bradford notes: "Al-Tabari (c. 870) recognizes that the only authentic interpretation of the above passage is that '. . . the likeness of Jesus was projected onto a single volunteer while Jesus safely exited through the roof of a house where the disciples had gathered. As a result, those who saw the crucifixion were confused because, in reality, the Jews did not kill Jesus; he only appeared to have died.' This version became the accepted Muslim tradition because al-Tabari traced the account to Ibn al-Abbas (d. c. 687), who had been a companion of Muhammad himself" (*Muhammad's Jesus*, 116).

55 Irenaeus of Lyons, *Against Heresies*, 1, 24, 4.

56 However, if everything is taken absolutely literally and without the use of any literary devices, then how is one to interpret those passages where Allah is described anthropomorphically, such as when the Quran speaks of Allah's face (55:26–27), hand (s48:10), eye (20:36–39), and shin (68:42)?

57 Standard Arabic-English lexicons define *makr* as involving a ruse or deception. English translations of the Quran almost universally translate *makr* as "plotting" or "scheming." One exception is the Muhammad Ahmed-Samira, which translates these verses as follows: "And they cheated/deceived and God cheated/deceived, and God is the best of the cheaters/deceivers" (3:54). Also see Quran 8:30.

58 If anything, it is our experience of God's will and not an attribute or quality of God. The case of the substitution of someone other than Jesus for crucifixion certainly would be an example of divine deception.

59 Robert R. Reilly, *The Closing of the Muslim Mind: How Intellectual Suicide Created the Modern Islamist Crisis* (Wilmington, DE: Intercollegiate Studies Institute, 2011), 30-34.

60 Id., 30.

61 "Nothing of our revelation (even a single verse) do we abrogate or cause be forgotten, but we bring (in place) one better or the like thereof. Knowest thou not that Allah is able to do all things?" (2:106). (see also 16:101.) Pickthall, *The Quran.*

62 *Stanford Encyclopedia of Philosophy*, Winter 2016, s.v. "Al-Ghazali," https://plato.stanford.edu/archives/win2016/entries/al-ghazali.

63 Reilly, *The Closing of the Muslim Mind,* 78.

64 Id., 64.

65 Ibid.

66 Ibid.

67 Id., 111-112.

68 Id. 147.

69 Basil, *Letter 204.6,* in *A Select Library of the Nicene and Post-Nicene Fathers of the Christian Church,* eds. Philip Schaff and Henry Wace, trans. Blomfield Jackson, vol. 8, *St. Basil: Letters and Select Works* (New York: The Christian Literature Company, 1895), 245.

70 Johann Peter Kirsch, "Pope John XII," in *The Catholic Encyclopedia*, eds. Charles Herbermann, Edward Pace, Condé Pallen, Thomas Shahan, and John Wynne, vol. 8 (New York: Robert Appleton Company, 1910), http://www.newadvent.org/cathen/08426b.htm.

71 Fourth Lateran Council, Denzinger 428.

72 From Trasancos, "The Stillbirth of Science in Greece," referencing Stanley Jaki's *A Late Awakening and Other Essays* (New Hope, KY: Real View Books, 2006), 50.

73 Tom Woods, "A Gift From the Middle Ages," LewRockwell.com, May 16, 2005, https://www.lewrockwell.com/2005/05/thomas-woods/a-gift-from-the-middle-ages/.

74 Ibid.

75 Id., 24-25.

76 Arnold Lunn, *Flight from Reason* (London: Eyre & Spottiswoode, 1932), 29.

77 This work corrects Averroes's interpretation of Aristotle regarding the possible intellect, which Averroes believed was in no way united

to the body as its form, and therefore the possible intellect is one for all men. See Aquinas, *De unitate intellectus contra Averroistas* (On the Uniqueness of the Intellect Against Averroists (1270) at https://isidore. co/aquinas/english/DeUnitateIntellectus.htm).

78   Aquinas, *On the Uniqueness of the Intellect Against Averroists*, section 122.

79   These condemnations speak directly to the arts faculty, so other departments could use the works of Aristotle. Also, the condemnations were for the University of Paris alone.

80   There are also condemnations aimed at some propositions by Thomas Aquinas. The condemnations against these are later lifted.

81   James J. Walsh and Thomas Williams, *Philosophy in the Middle Ages: The Christian, Islamic, and Jewish Traditions* (Indianapolis: Hackett Publishing Company, 2010), 541.

82   Scott Hahn and Benjamin Wiker, *Politicizing the Bible: The Roots of Historical Criticism and the Secularization of Scripture 1300-1700* (Freiburg im Breisgau: Herder & Herder Books, 2013), 25.

83   Michael Allen Gillespie, *Nihilism before Nietzsche* (Chicago: University of Chicago Press, 1996), 15.

84   Id., 17.

85   Ibid.

86   Id., 18-19.

87   Ibid.

88   "Ockham in this sense represents the first step on the road to the insight that faith alone is the basis of salvation." Id., 20-21.

89   Hahn and Wiker, *Politicizing the Bible*, 51.

90   Gillespie, *Nihilism Before Nietzsche*, 21.

91   "The rejection of realism and the assertion of radical individuality, beings could no longer be conceived as members of species or genera with a certain nature or potentiality. In Aristotelian terms, the rejection of formal causes was also the rejection of final causes. As a result, only material and efficient causality remained. The relations between the various material beings can be determined only by efficient causality and this causality can be known only by observation. Moreover, since each event is the result of the meeting of two unique entities, no necessary generalizations are possible. Therefore, science at best can be merely hypothetical." Ibid.

92   Id., 22.

93   William Turner, "William of Ockham," in *The Catholic Encyclopedia*, eds. Charles Herbermann, Edward Pace, Condé Pallen, Thomas Shahan, and John Wynne, vol. 15 (New York: Robert Appleton Company, 1912), http://www.newadvent.org/cathen/15636a.htm.

94 J.C. Robertson, *History of the Christian Church*, vol. 4 (London: John Murray, 1873), 103.
95 Karl Adams, *Roots of the Reformation*, trans. Cecily Hastings (Zanesville, OH: CHResources, 2013), loc. 123, Kindle.
96 Ibid.
97 Id., loc. 235–239.
98 Ibid.
99 Id., loc. 472.
100 Hahn and Wiker, *Politicizing the Bible*, 158.
101 "No phrase reveals so clearly the hidden evil that was to spoil the fruit of the Reformation than Luther's saying that Ockham was the only scholastic who was any good. The truth is that Luther, brought up on his system, was never able to think outside the framework it imposed, while this, it is only too evident, makes the mystery that lies at the root of Christian teaching either inconceivable or absurd." Louis Bouyer, *The Spirit and Forms of Protestantism* (London: The Harvill Press Ltd., 1956), 184.
102 *D. Martin Luthers Werke: Kritische Gesamtausgabe, Abteilung Werke,* ed. Ulrich Köpf, vol. 1 (Weimar, Ausgabe 1883-), 6.195, 4f, quoted in Oberman, *Man Between God and the Devil* (New Haven, CT: Yale University Press, 1989), 120. Emphasis mine.
103 Hahn and Wiker, *Politicizing the Bible*, 149–150.
104 Adams, *Roots of the Reformation*, loc. 552.
105 Martin Luther, *Luther's Works, Vol. 26: Lectures on Galatians, 1535, Chapters 1-4*, eds. Jaroslav Jan Pelikan, Hilton C. Oswald, and Helmut T. Lehmann (Saint Louis: Concordia Publishing House, 1999), 232–233.
106 Luther, Martin. *Luther's Works, Vol. 33: Career of the Reformer III*, eds. Jaroslav Jan Pelikan, Hilton C. Oswald, and Helmut T. Lehmann. Philadelphia: Fortress Press, 1999, 64.
107 Hartman Grisar, *Luther*, trans. E.M. Lamond (Freiburg im Breisgau: B. Herder, 1915), vol. 4, 3–4.
108 Ibid.
109 Ibid.
110 Ibid.
111 Martin Luther, *Luther's Works, Vol. 31: Career of the Reformer I.* Eds. Jaroslav Jan Pelikan, Hilton C. Oswald, and Helmut T. Lehmann. Philadelphia: Fortress Press, 1999, 297. Emphasis mine.
112 Luther, *Luther's Works, Vol. 31: Career of the Reformer I*, 351.
113 Ibid.
114 Paul Hacker, *Faith in Luther: Martin Luther and the Origin of*

Anthropocentric Religion (Steubenville, OH: Emmaus Academic, 2017), FN 9.

115 Martin Luther, *Luther's Works, Vol. 16: Lectures on Isaiah: Chapters 1-39*. Eds. Jaroslav Jan Pelikan, Hilton C. Oswald, and Helmut T. Lehmann. (Saint Louis: Concordia Publishing House, 1999), 136.

116 There is one example in Luther's writings where he expounds on apostolic Tradition in a way close to that of Catholicism: "Furthermore, when Christ commands his apostles to proclaim his word and to carry on his work, we hear and see him himself, and thus also God the Father; for they publish and proclaim no other word than that which they heard from his lips, and they point solely to him. Thus the process goes on; the word is handed down to us through the agency of true bishops, pastors, and preachers, who received it from the apostles. In this way all sermons delivered in Christendom must proceed from this one Christ; and the clergy must prove that the words and works of their ministry in Christendom—regardless of whether their own person is good or evil—are those of Christ. They must declare: 'You are not to look to me or to follow me. No, heed only that which the Lord Christ says to you or shows you through me; for this is not my word; it is Christ's word. The baptism and sacrament I administer is not mine; it is his baptism and sacrament. The office I fill is not mine; it is the Lord's office.'"

The footnote to this passage states that this is not the usual way Luther expounds on apostolic Tradition. Martin Luther, *Luther's Works, Vol. 24: Sermons on the Gospel of St. John: Chapters 14-16*. Eds. Jaroslav Jan Pelikan, Hilton C. Oswald, and Helmut T. Lehmann. (Saint Louis: Concordia Publishing House, 1999), 66.

117 Augustine, *On Christian Doctrine*, 2, 12. Emphasis mine.

118 Martin Luther, *Luther's Works, Vol. 35: Word and Sacrament I*. Eds. Jaroslav Jan Pelikan, Hilton C. Oswald, and Helmut T. Lehmann (Philadelphia: Fortress Press, 1999), 396. Emphasis mine. Whom did the "we" refer to if not the apostles Peter, James, and John? It certainly didn't refer to Judas, Annas, Pilate, and Herod.

119 Id., 150.

120 T.G. Tappert, *The Book of Concord: The Confessions of the Evangelical Lutheran Church* (Philadelphia: Fortress Press, 2000), 332.

121 Martin Luther, *Luther's Works, Vol. 44: The Christian in Society I*. Eds. Jaroslav Jan Pelikan, Hilton C. Oswald, and Helmut T. Lehmann (Philadelphia: Fortress Press, 1999), 128.

122 Martin Luther, *Luther's Works, Vol. 36: Word and Sacrament II*. Eds. Jaroslav Jan Pelikan, Hilton C. Oswald, and Helmut T. Lehmann

(Philadelphia: Fortress Press, 1999), 117.

123 John Henry Newman, *Lectures on Justification* (Miami: HardPress, 2018), lecture 1, 4.

124 D. *Martin Luthers Werke. Kritsche Gesamtausgabe* (Weimar: Herman Bohlaus Nachfolger, 1883), 36, 416–477. English translation by Jim Anderson (unpublished).

125 Brian Moynahan, *The Faith: A History of the Christian Faith* (New York: Image Books, 2003), 375.

126 Martin Luther, *Luther's Works, Vol. 32: Career of the Reformer II*. Eds. Jaroslav Jan Pelikan, Hilton C. Oswald, and Helmut T. Lehmann (Philadelphia: Fortress Press, 1999), 112–113. The footnote to this passage states: "These words are given in German in the Latin text upon which this translation is based. There is good evidence, however, that Luther actually said only: 'May God help me!' Cf. *Deutsche Reichstagsakten*, Vol. II: *Deutsche Reichstagsakten unter Kaiser Karl V* (Gotha, 1896), 587." Emphasis mine.

127 As quoted in M. Michelet's *The Life of Luther Gathered from His Own Writings*, trans. G. H. Smith (New Kensignton, PA: Whittaker and Co., n.d.), 91–92

128 Vincent of Lérins, *Commonitory*, 2, 5.

129 Martin Luther, *Luther's Works, Vol. 45: The Christian in Society II*. Eds. Jaroslav Jan Pelikan, Hilton C. Oswald, and Helmut T. Lehmann. (Philadelphia: Fortress Press, 1999), 91.

130 *Catalogus Testium Veritatis, Qui Ante Nostram Aetatem Pontifici Romano Eiusque Erroribus Reclamarunt* (Basel: Joannem Oporinum, 1556).

131 "An Ecclesiastical History, embracing the whole idea of the Church of Christ, pertaining to as much as the Place, Propagation, Persecution, Tranquility, Doctrine, Heresies, Ceremonies, Government, Schisms, Synods, People, Miracles, Martyrs, Rites outside of the Church, and the political situation of the empire, [sorted] in clearly visible order by single centuries: having been compiled with remarkable diligence and faith from the most ancient and best historians, patriarchs, and other writers: By some dedicated and pious men in the city of Magdeburg."

132 Edward Myers, "Centuriators of Madeburg," in *The Catholic Encyclopedia*, eds. Charles Herbermann, Edward Pace, Condé Pallen, Thomas Shahan, and John Wynne, vol. 3 (New York: Robert Appleton Company, 1908), http://www.newadvent.org/cathen/03534b.htm.

133 Ibid.

134 The "Pope Joan" myth propounds that in the tenth century, a woman hid her sex and was ordained a priest, created a cardinal, and

eventually elected pope. Her deceit was discovered when she gave birth during a papal procession, where she was subsequently stoned. The myth is medieval, predating Protestantism, and has no grounds for belief. See Patrick Madrid's *Pope Fiction: Answers to 30 Myths and Misconceptions About the Papacy* (Rancho Santa Fe, CA: Basilica Press, 2000), 167-177.

135 *Ecclesiastical Annals from Christ's Nativity to the Year 1198.*

136 Ludwig Ott, *Fundamentals of Catholic Dogma* (Freiburg im Breisgau: B. Herder Book Company, 1957), 160. Also see *Formula of Concord: Ep, art.* viii, *par.* 11.

137 Timothy George, *Theology of the Reformers* (Nashville: B&H Publishing Group, 2013), 157-158.

138 Alister McGrath, *Twilight of Atheism: The Rise and Fall of Disbelief in Modern World* (New York: Doubleday, 2004), 202-203.

139 Hans Boersma, *Heavenly Participation: The Weaving of a Sacramental Tapestry* (Grand Rapids, MI: Wm. B. Eerdmans Publishing, 2011), 92-93.

140 See Calvin's *Sermon on Job*, 415 and *Bondage and Liberation of the Will*, 148.

141 Susan E. Schreiner, *Where Shall Wisdom be Found?: Calvin's Exegesis of Job from Medieval and Modern Perspectives* (Chicago: University of Chicago Press, 2017), 113.

142 Hans Boersma, *Violence, Hospitality, and the Cross: Reappropriating the Atonement Tradition* (Ada, MI: Baker Academic, 2006), 61.

143 Calvin, *Institutes*, 3, 24, 8.

144 Robin Philips, "Why I Stopped Being a Calvinist—A Deformed Christology (Part 5)," Orthodoxy and Heterodoxy, Ancient Faith Ministries, January 23, 2014, https://blogs.ancientfaith.com/orthodoxyandheterodoxy/2014/01/23/why-i-stopped-being-a-calvinist-part-5-a-deformed-christology.

145 Tending to perfection refers to Christ in his humanity. It is in this sense that Christ "learned obedience through what he suffered" (Heb. 5:8). Also see Gregory of Nazianzus (*Orat.* 30.6).

146 Calvin, *Institutes*, 2, 17, 1.

147 Philips, "Why I Stopped Being a Calvinist."

148 F. Bruce Gordon, *Calvin* (New Haven, CT: Yale University Press, 2009), 137.

149 Florimond de Raemond, *Histoire de la naissance, progrez et decadence de l'hérésie de ce siècle* (Rouen: Chez P. La Motte, 1628-1629), 999; cited in Thomas Lambert, "Preaching, Praying and Policing the Reform in Sixteenth-Century Geneva" (Ph.D. diss., University of

Wisconsin, Madison, 1998), 280, quoted in David Anders's "Have You Been Born Again? Catholic Reflections on a Protestant Doctrine, or How Calvin's View of Salvation Destroyed His Doctrine of the Church," Called to Communion, March 14, 2012, https://www.calledtocommunion.com/2012/03/have-you-been-born-again-catholic-reflections-on-a-protestant-doctrine-or-how-calvins-view-of-salvation-destroyed-his-doctrine-of-the-church.

150 William A. Dyrness, *Poetic Theology: God and the Poetics of Everyday Life* (Grand Rapids, MI: Wm. B. Eerdmans, 2011), 223.

151 Sermon, preached Tuesday, December 25, 1551, *Sermons on the Book of Micah*, trans. Benjamin W. Farley (Phillipsburg, NJ: P&R Publishing, 2003), 302-304.

152 Alister McGrath, *Twilight of Atheism: The Rise and Fall of Disbelief in the Modern World*, (Colorado Springs: Waterbrook, 2006), 203.

153 Chris Coldwell, "John Calvin and Holy Days," Naphtali Press, https://www.naphtali.com/articles/chris-coldwell/john-calvin-and-holy-days.

154 Stephanie Mann, *Supremacy and Survival: How Catholics Endured the English Reformation* (Strongsville, OH: Scepter Publishers, 2018), loc. 1379, Kindle.

155 Francis Aidan Cardinal Gasquet, "Suppression of English Monasteries under Henry VIII," in *The Catholic Encyclopedia*, eds. Charles Herbermann, Edward Pace, Condé Pallen, Thomas Shahan, and John Wynne, vol. 10 (New York: Robert Appleton Company, 1911), http://www.newadvent.org/cathen/10455a.htm.

156 Ibid.

157 Ibid.

158 Sidney & Beatrice Webb, *English Local Government: English Poor Law History*, vol. 1 (London: Longmans, Green, and Company, 1927), 48.

159 See "The Poor Laws," Witheridge, http://www.witheridge-historical-archive.com/poor-1.htm.

160 James Bonar, *Malthus and His Work* (Miami: HardPress, 2018), 332.

161 The title of his book is *Population Bomb, The Population Control or Race to Oblivion* (New York: Ballantine Books).

162 Herbert Butterfield, *The Whig Interpretation of History* (New York: W.W. Norton & Company, 1965), 5.

163 Id., 18.

164 Christoph Rasperger, *Ducentae paucorum istorum, et quidem clarissimorum Christi verborum: Hoc est Corpus meum; interpretations* (Ingolstadt: A. Weissenhorn, 1577).

165 Brad S. Gregory, *Unintended Reformation: How a Religious Revolution*

Secularized Society (Cambridge, MA: The Belknap of Harvard University Press, 2012), loc. 3481, Kindle.

166 Hahn and Wiker, *Politicizing the Bible*, 181.

167 William T. Cavanaugh, *The Myth of Religious Violence: Secular Ideology and the Roots of Modern Conflict* (Oxford: Oxford University Press, 2009), 72.

168 Lord Herbert of Cherbury, *The Ancient Religion of the Gentiles, and Causes of Their Errors*, 3-4.

169 Cavanaugh, *The Myth of Religious Violence*, 75.

170 Id., 77.

171 *Summa Theologica* II-II, Q. 80, 1.

172 Cavanaugh, *The Myth of Religious Violence*, 68.

173 Id., 69.

174 Ibid.

175 Craig S. Keener, *Miracles* vol. 1 (Ada, MI: Baker Academic, 2011), 374.

176 Edward Rues, *History of the Canon of the Holy Scriptures in the Christian Church*, trans. David Hunter (Edinburgh: James Gemmell, George IV. Bridge, 1884), 361-362.

177 See section 10 of his "An Enquiry concerning Human Understanding."

178 See *Calvinism and Religious Toleration in the Dutch Golden Age*, eds. R. Po-Chia Hsia and Henk Van Nierop (Cambridge, MA: Cambridge University Press, 2002).

179 "Strongly desirous of acquiring and possessing" (*Merriam-Webster*, s.v. "acquisitive," https://www.merriam-webster.com/dictionary/acquisitive).

180 John Locke, "A Letter Concerning Toleration," trans. William Popple (London: 1689).

181 Cavanaugh, *The Myth of Religious Violence*, 80.

182 Id., 83.

183 Id. Emphasis his.

184 Nathaniel Micklem, *National Socialism and the Roman Catholic Church: Being an Account of the Conflict between the National Socialist Government of Germany and the Roman Catholic Church, 1933-1938* (Oxford: Oxford University Press, 1939), 2. Emphasis mine.

185 Brad S. Gregory, *The Unintended Reformation: How a Religious Revolution Secularized Society* (Cambridge, MA: The Belknap Press of Harvard University Press), 2012, loc. 1243, Kindle.

186 See "Flew on Hume on miracles," Edward Feser, http://edwardfeser.blogspot.com/2017/09/flew-on-hume-on-miracles.html.

187 Gregory, *The Unintended Reformation*, loc. 6974.

188 For example, *The Westminster Confession of Faith*, 18, 2 points out
     several of these.
189 Mark Noll, *America's God: From Jonathan Edwards to Abraham Lincoln,*
     (Oxford: Oxford University Press, 2002), 24.
190 Anders, "Have You Been Born Again?"
191 Noll, *America's God*, 32-34.
192 Id., 43.
193 *Journals* (Edinburgh: Banner of Truth, 1960), 458, cited in Mark Noll,
     The Rise of Evangelicalism: The Age of Edwards, Whitefield and the Wesleys
     (Downers Grove, IL: IVP, 2003), 13-15, as quoted in Anders, "Have
     You Been Born Again?"
194 Ibid.
195 Ibid.
196 See Arthur and Theresa Beem's *It's OK Not to Be a Seventh-Day
     Adventist* (Charleston, SC: BookSurge Publishing, 2008) for details on
     this devastation.
197 See E.G. White's *The Great Controversy.*
198 Robert S. Cox, *Body and Soul: A Sympathetic History of American
     Spiritualism* (Charlottesville, VA: University of Virginia Press, 2003),
     237.
199 Charles Filmore and James Tierney, *Metaphysical Bible Dictionary*
     (Mineola, NY: Dover Publications, Inc., 2013), 151.
200 Charles Darwin, *The Descent of Man, and Selection in Relation to Sex,*
     vol. 1 (London: John Murray, 1871), 168. Emphasis mine.
201 Ibid. Emphasis mine.
202 Advertisement in the *Birth Control Review* 1, no. 1 (New series,
     October 1933): 8.
203 *The Pivot of Civilization in Historical Perspective: The Birth Control Classic,*
     eds. Michael Perry, Margaret Sanger, H.G. Wells (n.p.: Inkling Books,
     2001), 322.
204 Ibid.
205 Ernst Rudin. "Eugenic Sterilization: An Urgent Need," *Birth Control
     Review* 27, no. 4 (April 1933): 102–104.
206 "People with Disabilities," United States Holocaust Memorial
     Museum, https://www.ushmm.org/collections/bibliography/people-
     with-disabilities.
207 John William Draper, *History of the Conflict Between Religion and Science*
     (New York: D. Appleton and Co., 1898), 6.
208 Ibid.
209 David Lindberg and Ronald Numbers, *God and Nature: Historical
     Essays on the Encounter Between Christianity and Science* (Berkeley, CA:

University of California Press, 1986), 2-3.

210 See Ludwig Ott's *Fundamentals of Catholic Dogma*, 93ff, for an explanation of what the Church has dogmatically defined with regard to evolution and special creation.

211 See *Summa Contra Gentiles*, chs. 71, 72, 74, and 77.

212 William Bouwsma, *John Calvin: A Sixteenth-Century Portrait* (Oxford: Oxford University Press, 1987), 165-166. Emphasis his.

213 Rev. C.G. Finney, "Regeneration" (speech, Borough Road Chapel, Southwark, UK, November 21, 1849).

214 As quoted in Anders's "Have you been Born Again?".

215 "From the *Babylonian Captivity of the Church* to the end of his life— though with the significant exception of his Lectures on Genesis, in which he named marriage as another 'estate' apart from temporal authority—Luther would insist that marriage was a matter for the temporal kingdom, and thus its regulation fell under the jurisdiction of the secular authorities rather than under the clergy as a sacrament" (Jarrett A. Carty, *God and Government: Martin Luther's Political Thought* [Chicago: McGill-Queen's University, 2017], 147).

216 For example, *Westminster Confession*, 24.6.

217 Anders, "Have You Been Born Again?"

218 Ed Stetzer, "The Rapid Rise of Nondenominational Christianity: My Most recent Piece at CNN," *Christianity Today*, June 12, 2015, https://www.christianitytoday.com/edstetzer/2015/june/rapid-rise-of-non-denominational-christianity-my-most-recen.html.

219 Ron Roizen, "Utilitarianism as Part of the English Moral Philosophical Tradition," God and the English Utilitarians (IV), The Victorian Web, http://www.victorianweb.org/philosophy/roizen/4.html.

220 Ibid.

221 *Summa Contra Gentiles*, 3.34.

222 For example, the Mauryan dynasty of India (c. 321-c. 185 B.C.), the Qin dynasty of China (221-207 B.C.), and the reign of Chief Shaka among the Zulu tribes (c. 1816-28).

223 R.J. Rummel, *Death by Government* (New Brunswick, NJ: Transaction Publishers, 1994), accessed at https://www.hawaii.edu/powerkills/NOTE1.HTM.

224 See Helge Kragh's "Science and Ideology: The Case of Cosmology in the Soviet Union, 1947-1963," *Acta Baltica Historiae et Philosophiae Scientiarum* 1, 1 (Spring 2013), 35–58.

225 "Address to the Houston Ministers Conference" (speech, Greater Houston Ministerial Association, Houston, TX, September 12,

1960). Transcript at https://www.npr.org/templates/story/story.
php?storyId=16920600.

226 Anne Hendershott, "Taking the Catholic Out of Catholic
Universities," City Journal (Autumn 2017), https://www.city-journal.
org/html/taking-catholic-out-catholic-universities-15495.html.

227 Theodore Hesburgh ed., *The Challenge and Promise of the Catholic
University* (Notre Dame, IN: University of Notre Dame Press, 1994).

228 See Peter M. Mitchell's *The Coup at Catholic University: The 1968
Revolution in American Catholic Education* (San Francisco: Ignatius Press,
2015).

229 Sue Ellen Browder, *Sex and the Catholic Feminist: New Choices for a New
Generation* (San Francisco: Ignatius Press, 2020), 30.

230 *Gospel of Thomas*, logion 114.

231 Simone de Beauvoir, *The Second Sex* (New York: Vintage Books,
2011), 24.

232 See Sue Ellen Browder's *Subverted* (San Francisco: Ignatius Press,
2015), and *Sex and the Catholic Feminist*.

233 "Divorce and Death: Their Social & Social-Psychological Impacts,"
Michael C. Kearl, Trinity University, http://faculty.trinity.edu/
mkearl/fam-div.html.

234 Janet P. Simmons, "No Fault Divorce Is Faulty Indeed," *Silicon Valley
Business Journal*, September 8, 1996, https://www.bizjournals.com/
sanjose/stories/1996/09/09/editorial4.html.

235 Daniel Davis, "50 Years of No-Fault Divorce Gave Us a Throwaway
Culture," CNSNews, Media Research Center, September 5, 2019,
https://www.cnsnews.com/commentary/daniel-davis/50-years-no-
fault-divorce-gave-us-throwaway-culture.

236 Andrew Blake, "Satanic prayer opens Pensacola city council meeting;
police forced to remove protesters," *The Washington Times*, July 15,
2016, https://www.washingtontimes.com/news/2016/jul/15/satanic-
prayer-opens-pensacola-city-council-meetin.

237 Planned Parenthood v. Casey, 505 U.S. 833 (1992).

238 Pope St. John XXIII, *Gaudium et Spes* [On the Church in the Modern
World], Vatican II, December 7, 1965, 36.

239 Adolf Hitler, *Mein Kampf* (Boston, MA: Houghton Mifflin, 1969), 134.

240 Pope Francis, Message for World Communications Day (January
24, 2018), https://www.vatican.va/content/francesco/en/messages/
communications/documents/papa-francesco_20180124_messaggio-
comunicazioni-sociali.html.

241 "The 'Loneliness Epidemic,'" Health Resources & Services
Administration, https://www.hrsa.gov/enews/past-issues/2019/

january-17/loneliness-epidemic.

242 "An Epidemic of Loneliness," The Week, Dennis Publishing Limited, January 6, 2019, https://theweek.com/articles/815518/epidemic-loneliness.

243 Ibid.

244 Kristine Phillips, "A mother married her son and then her daughter, who just pleaded guilty to incest, officials say," *The Washington Post*, November 11, 2017 https://www.washingtonpost.com/news/true-crime/wp/2017/11/11/a-mother-married-her-son-and-then-her-daughter-who-just-pleaded-guilty-to-incest-officials-say.

245 Cydney Henderson, "Jameela Jamil cancels Candace Owens' appearance after 'only women can give birth' tweet," *USA Today*, January 3, 2020 https://www.usatoday.com/story/entertainment/celebrities/2020/01/03/jameela-jamil-cancels-candace-owens-podcast-appearance-after-tweet/2801895001.

246 Flew explains his decision to abandon atheism in the book. Antony Flew and Roy Abraham Varghese, *There Is a God: How the World's Most Notorious Atheist Changed His Mind* (San Francisco: HarperOne, 2008).

247 Francis Beckwith, "Philosophy and Belief in God: The Resurgence of Theism in Philosophical Circles," *The Master's Seminary* 2, no. 1 (Spring 1991): 61–77 https://www.tms.edu/msj/msj2-1-4.

248 Reilly, *The Closing of the Muslim Mind*, 11.

249 Camino pilgrimage statistics accessed at Camino Pilgrim, The Confraternity of St. James, https://www.csj.org.uk.